Songs of Yemaya

stories of black womanhood

An anthology
Edited by Nichelle Marie Calhoun

With contributions from women throughout the Diaspora

Songs of Yemaya

stories of black womanhood

Copyright © 2017 by Nichelle M. Calhoun

All rights reserved. This book or any portion thereof may not be reproduced or used in any manner whatsoever without the express written permission of the publisher except for the use of brief quotations in a book review.

ISBN 978-0-692-92043-5

Published by
Diaspora Records
13111 Larchdale Laurel, MD 20707
www.songsofyemaya.com

Cover Illustration by Diana Lane
dandjlane@gmail.com
https://www.behance.net/dandjlane

Photo Credit for Destiny Hemphill @ Zaina Alsous

Black Death by Melissa Dunmore
Originally published in *Black Lives Have Always Mattered*
2Leaf Press, 2017

Lost Love by Althea Romeo-Mark
Originally Published in *Women in War: (Protest Against Gender Violence)*
CWC, Gambia 2015

Yemaya-Olokun and *A Tale Based on Olokun's Inspiration* by Luisah Teish
Originally Published in *Jambalaya: The Woman's Natural Book of Personal Charms and Practical Rituals*
HarperCollins Publishers, 1988

Songs of Yemaya

stories of black womanhood

To motherhood, and purpose...

DEDICATION

Dedicated to Black Womanhood
(Irrespective of time and space)

Whose strength is only rivaled by its softness
Whose resistance is all-encompassing
Whose tears have borne new nations
Whose embrace has outarmed supremacy
Whose womb has carried a world

These are your songs.

For both Emmas, Jackie, Joyce, Jasmine, and Lillian

Songs of Yemaya

stories of black womanhood

An anthology
Edited by Nichelle Marie Calhoun
With contributions from women throughout the Diaspora

Kehryse Vanessa Johnson
Lise-May Arnal
Melissa Dunmore
Queen Ella Zuree
Catherine Toppin
Christiana Harrell
Cherise Charleswell
Radhiyah Ayobami
Juanita Cox
Jimmie Ware
L'Angela Honeysuckle Moon Lee
Luisah Teish
NLisah
Nefertiti Asanti
Lusungu Kayani-Stearns
Celeta Hickman
Tania Saintil (Deliverance-NOIRE)
Althea Romeo-Mark
Rashida James-Saadiya
Sileta Blu Hodge
Destiny Hemphill
Andria Nacina Cole
Donna McGregor Hall
Janine Jackson

CONTENTS

Introduction 1

Your womanhood is your domain. Make sure you are the author of its laws.

Renée in Wild Revolt by Kehryse Vanessa Johnson 9
Strength of Songs by Lise-May Arnal 16
Memories like Mammaries by Melissa Dunmore 18
Shattered by Queen Ella Zuree 20
Err on the Side of Over-Confidence by Catherine Toppin 22
Too Something by Lise-May Arnal 25
Like Coffee by Christiana Harrell...28
There is NO Gap by Cherise Charleswell 33
Under the Veil by Radhiyah Ayobami 36

I got sisters in different area codes.

Manifesto by Radhiyah Ayobami 38
We Were Born on a Sunday by Juanita Cox................................43
Black She by Melissa Dunmore 44
Our Glorious Truth by Jimmie Ware 50

The universe is in your mother's womb. It is equipped with all that you need.

Mami Wata Cradles by Juanita Cox 53
Spirit of Woman by L'Angela Honeysuckle Moon Lee 58
Yemaya-Olokun by Luisah Teish 62
Passing Down by Nichelle Marie Calhoun 64
A Tale Based on Olokun's Inspiration by Luisah Teish 68
We Learned, They Taught, I Teach by NLisah 70

Single MOM-NESS by Queen Ella Zuree 73

Sensuality is loving the details of living.
Kin to Night Music by Nefertiti Asanti 75
Morning Song by Lusungu Kayani-Stearns 77
Young Yemaya 7 Oceans of Blue by Celeta Hickman 79
The Making of a Woman by Lise-May Arnal... 80
Spoken Hands by Tania Saintil (Deliverance-NOIRE)............................. 82

The answer is in the middle of it.
Lost Love by Althea Romeo-Mark 85
Summer Story by Melissa Dunmore 87
Self-Preservation Love Notes by Rashida James-Saadiya........................ 90
A Survivor's Dilemma by Cherise Charleswell... 92
Thelonius Monk Plays Again by Tania Saintil (Deliverance-NOIRE).... 93

Maybe you are already full.
The Familiar Ways of Broken People by Nefertiti Asanti........................ 96
Nana's Daughters by Sileta Blu Hodge... 98
So the Ship Was Likely to Be Broken by Destiny Hemphill................... 116
40 and . . . by Lise-May Arnal 119

Stay free.
The Gorgeous Word NO by Andria Nacina Cole 123
ENCOMIUM: A Manumitted Scream by Lise-May Arnal..................... 125
Black Death by Melissa Dunmore... 126
If Not You - Then Who?! by NLisah 129
I Know a Burning Bush When I See One by Destiny Hemphill 130
Redemption of Mammy by Celeta Hickman 132
Black by Donna McGregor Hall.. 134
Recalling Origins: The Blending of Blue Waters by Celeta Hickman ..135
Yemaya by Janine Jackson 138

ACKNOWLEDGMENTS

Maferefún

Special acknowledgments to the featured authors and artists who entrusted me with the honor of their voices, and the opportunity to record their experiences through their lenses. Additional acknowledgments to Trelani Duncan, who helped build the foundation of this project, and inspired and propelled the project forward when I was at a standstill.

I deeply thank you all.

INTRODUCTION

Domestic. Domestic. Laborer. Domestic. Slave. It is a typical Friday night for me, thumbing through census documents by decade—eyes focused intently on the women before me, noting my literal forefathers as an afterthought. I find myself desperately trying to unravel the loc'd stories of the women with whom I share a bloodline, those who came before me. Rachel, Hattie, Hattie, Charlotte, Mary, Frances, Idella, Viverine, Polly. For most of the women, I have nothing more than birth and death dates; a listing of their households and head of households; the names of their husbands—my forefathers; their ability to read or write; and their varying racial classifications—Black, Colored, Negro, Mulatto, Mulatto, Negro—ever-changing superficial classifications that determined their fates, their access, their value in society, their visibility.

I routinely sit with these women, digging for just pieces of them. They are sacred—holy books with inspiration for living—and even though I know so little about them, I know that through all the macro and micro indignities of history, they continued. They are how I exist; therefore, I know they hold the key to supernatural survival in the most brutal, life-halting, life-grabbing situations. Most of my known foremothers were born so long ago that even the eldest members of my family have only heard of them in name. Mostly, never at all. Descendants bear namesakes without connection. Those bearing namesakes are shocked to hear my family reunion genealogical reports that reveal homage to someone born as far back as the 1800s. But these holy women live on in the legacy of their families, whether recognized or unrecognized. Their individual stories are largely silenced, lost in a narrative that shapes a time but not the individuals living within that time.

The stretches of my foremothers' lives varied. Based on the brief demographic data recorded in government documents, some had lives abbreviated by illness or premature death while others lived with enviable longevity given known systemic oppression. They were mothers, aunts, daughters, sisters, and widows. They were single, married, maybe even two-spirit, although not captured in the data. Some had been sold or had children taken from their arms. Some grew up in locales that family had lived in for generations. Some sought new lives via the Great Migration.

Whatever their bare bones demographic indications recorded in history, they are giants to me.

Even reading the skeletal demographics of their lives, they rise up off the page, share my space, my thoughts, my life—and propel me to tell the stories of black women. It is in this process that I began to imagine an anthology that traveled the inner landscapes of contemporary black women, highlighting their varied, intersectional experiences, capturing their voices and refuting the silence imposed on their foremothers. It is in this spirit that I honor the women whose voices were not captured, by grasping their legacies through the voices of their daughters.

Ironically, my personal relationship with black womanhood is a relatively recent shift. It began mostly in 2012, after seven years of living in Miami, Florida. I had returned to graduate school for a degree in Latin American and Caribbean Studies with a focus on the African Diaspora, and I had begun to take coursework in gender studies and global social-cultural studies. I initially moved to Miami in 2005 to pursue a graduate degree in international administration. At that time, I was determined to work in international development on the continent, specifically in West Africa, but didn't realize how much Miami would reshape me and bring West Africa to me in other ways.

I had gotten a part-time teaching job at Miami-Dade College in a primarily Cuban city called Hialeah. As one of the few Americans on staff, English became a secondary language on the daily, and Cuban culture became my living manual as I taught and befriended other Cubans. The opening of a new world fueled my love for the Diaspora, and by the time I returned to school for the second time, I had traveled extensively back and forth to the Latin American and Caribbean region for nearly a decade.

But my experiences while traveling as a black woman, as well as my racialized, genderized experiences in Miami, left me feeling as if I were missing a greater narrative. So, the return to graduate school was about discovery, and the discipline of anthropology offered me the tools in which to interpret my experiences in Miami, the United States, and Latin America and the Caribbean. Works, such as *Downtown Ladies: Informal Commercial Importers, a Haitian Anthropologist, and Self-Making in Jamaica* by Gina A. Ulysse; *Black Behind the Ears* by Ginetta

E.B. Candelario; *The Black Atlantic* by Paul Gilroy; and others, began to challenge my narrow, socially-constructed lens.

Mentally, I had entered graduate school a black person but left graduate school a black woman. I left with the tools to see and verbalize myself and my experiences. I began to interrogate the invisible and to teach my daughter to interrogate the invisible; the invisible became my focus. My world had always been filled with incredible black women: my mother, my great-aunts, my friends, their mothers—a network of dynamic women whom I saw but did not *see*. I had always learned that certain types of black womanhood were acceptable and those rules were always fluid, changing, restrictive. They were built on respectability politics that required constant outside approval.

My nascent connection to womanhood in color in that second stint in graduate school reordered me: my connection to my spirituality, my connection to the Diaspora, my connection to myself. With increased exposure, I learned about other faiths and spirituality via African-derived religions. An extended network of friends of the Yoruba faith in my adopted home of Miami continuously schooled me, opening up new windows of spirituality, breaking down the *Orishas* to me. I was beginning to learn my intersection with African deities and beginning to piece together childhood memories of my great-aunts, who continued to use *roots* as a way of life despite leaving their rural North Carolina home for Washington, D.C. The black church began to take on new wonder as I began to make connections to diasporic religions.

It was becoming overwhelmingly clear to me that while people of the African Diaspora were connected by the shared historical global experience of brutal repression, marginalization, and "invisibilization," they were also connected by the resilient, healing, soulful, and otherworldly dynamics that catapulted them beyond realities to survive and thrive, and that black women were at the very epicenter of that healing process.

I began to celebrate rather than shy away from the collection of our spirits meeting in safe spaces of unapologetic blackness. I began to notice black women laughing heartily, working the spirit through their bodies, pushing it up from their bellies to thrown-out backs. I began to note the spirit in knee-slapping and howling in musical octaves. I began to notice how we dance these spirits fiercely with strength and bravado or repeatedly in naturally measured step, how we perform them lightly and airily, all embodied lessons in human softness, fragility, strength, and the art of the "bounce back." I began to listen more acutely to the historical sounds of our ancestors, which we send through our vocal chords, in that way producing their spirits: soul music. I began to notice that the Diaspora speaks in a creolized language that says, *I know a part of you because a part of you is me.*

Children of the African Diaspora have truly worked the spirit much, and the spirit has, in turn, worked us. So I naturally moved toward the African deity Yemaya, not to privilege black motherhood as the central black woman experience, but rather to give credence to the fact that black motherhood is the cell of the world, and humanity rests in her womb. Life starts in the ocean, and healing-continued life, with saltwater.

I paid homage in proper order.

Yemaya, "source of all waters," was born in the West African Yoruba spiritual tradition in what today is Nigeria. Transported to the New World via the spirituality of the African ethnic groups taken captive during the Transatlantic slave trade, her name means "mother whose children are the fish." She wipes away sorrow, she comforts, and she angers slowly. She is invoked to bring clarity and tranquil seas, to remove obstacles to women, and to facilitate all things regarding motherhood.

In *Songs of Yemaya*, you see her saltwater presence cleansing and wiping away sorrow, healing, and celebrating continued life despite. Yemaya is represented by the moon in Brazil, Haiti, and other parts of the Americas. In the form of a mermaid in Haiti, she brings wealth and seduction. Her colors are blue and white. Her number is seven, which is represented in this anthology by its seven parts. She has many variations to her name: Mami Watta, Yemoja, La Sirene, Mommi, Nana Buruku, Iemanja, Iemaia, Yemalla, Ye-manja, and Yemoja, among others.

The women, the *yemayas*, who have submitted to this anthology provide the essence of this project. Their works are the trapbeat that rebooms in your car and liberates you after a dozen Monday microaggressions; they are the recipes for wiping away sorrow; they are the movement of water—steady and ongoing. The contributors exhibit the range of experiences, determining their own, grappling with socially constructed ideas, and challenging what restricts them. They dote on the moment, the sensuality of living, transition, change, acceptance, motherhood, love. They examine problematic societal norms and walk us through their journeys of becoming their individual brands of "woke." They guide us through their losses and revelations.

The works of Kehryse, Cherise, and Catherine take us to hard-won confidence reminding us of our power. They embody the protectiveness and directness of Yemaya—unapologetically reminding the reader that they are the ocean, forever coming and essential. Juanita and Luisah flesh out the spirit of Yemaya. Juanita's work realizes Yemaya through description, bringing her essence close while exploring diasporic consciousness and motherhood. Luisah brings the reader to the Pataki (the sacred stories of the *Orishas*), bringing the art of storytelling and the sacred together. Radhiyah, Christiana, and Rashida embrace themes of dominion over self as freedom and expression. NLisah speaks to intergenerational wisdom. All show the ever-evolving dynamism in pushing against societal expectations.

Melissa explores creolized identity, its connects and disconnects, and the problematic nature of authenticity narratives. Destiny and Melissa both wrestle with state-sanctioned violence and living in dual consciousness. Lise-May Arnal and Honeysuckle Moon evoke the senses and the ephemeral. Womanhood and change live in each line of their works. Sileta, Lusungu, and Queen Ella Zuree center motherhood. Deliverance-NOIRE exposes, removing the shame in silence. Jimmie Ware and Donna remind us of our refuge and strength. Nefertiti, Andria, and Destiny deal with heartbreak and its existential lessons. The artwork of Janine once again envelops us in the very essence of Yemaya. Althea asserts the theme of loss and country, a secondary diaspora, while Celeta's work speaks of healing and reclamation and praise of Yemaya.

In the years since I first embarked on this anthology, much has changed. The political climate of the United States, where most of the contributors hail from, has grown increasingly volatile as white supremacy has rejuvenated old forms of violence and revisited terrorism on the lives and psyches of black men, women, and children in new ways. Hashtags such as #BlackLivesMatter, #BlackGirlMagic, #SayHerName, #BlackWomenatWork, #BlackWomenDidThat, and #Melanin, amongst others, highlight the mixed challenges of a group in some ways boasting in achievement and pride but simultaneously reduced by the effects of institutional, ideological, and interpersonal racism and sexism.

Nevertheless, black women resist, persist, and assist in cleansing the world of its sorrow by widening the ways for social justice from the family unit to the streets to government.

The selected contributors to this anthology bring their songs, their stories, their tempests against the presumed call to order by white supremacy and male dominance in its varied shades. This book is a celebration of black womanhood in its most essential form—out of the voices of black women. These women are a part of the diverse, heterogeneous experiences of black womanhood.

The women of this anthology present their voices, their stories, their past and present and how it has informed their identity in black womanhood. In the seemingly genderless black struggle for racial equality, this book shares a drop of the stories to be told. The included poems, quotes, essays, stories and images reflect black women's skillful resistance despite constant efforts in reduction by racism, classism, misogyny, misogynoir, ageism, and homophobia.

Black women show up, carrying on nations, cleansing sorrow, protecting legacies, and "leaping like the tide."

Full like the oceans they are.

These are their songs.

Don't be afraid to visit me in the depths.

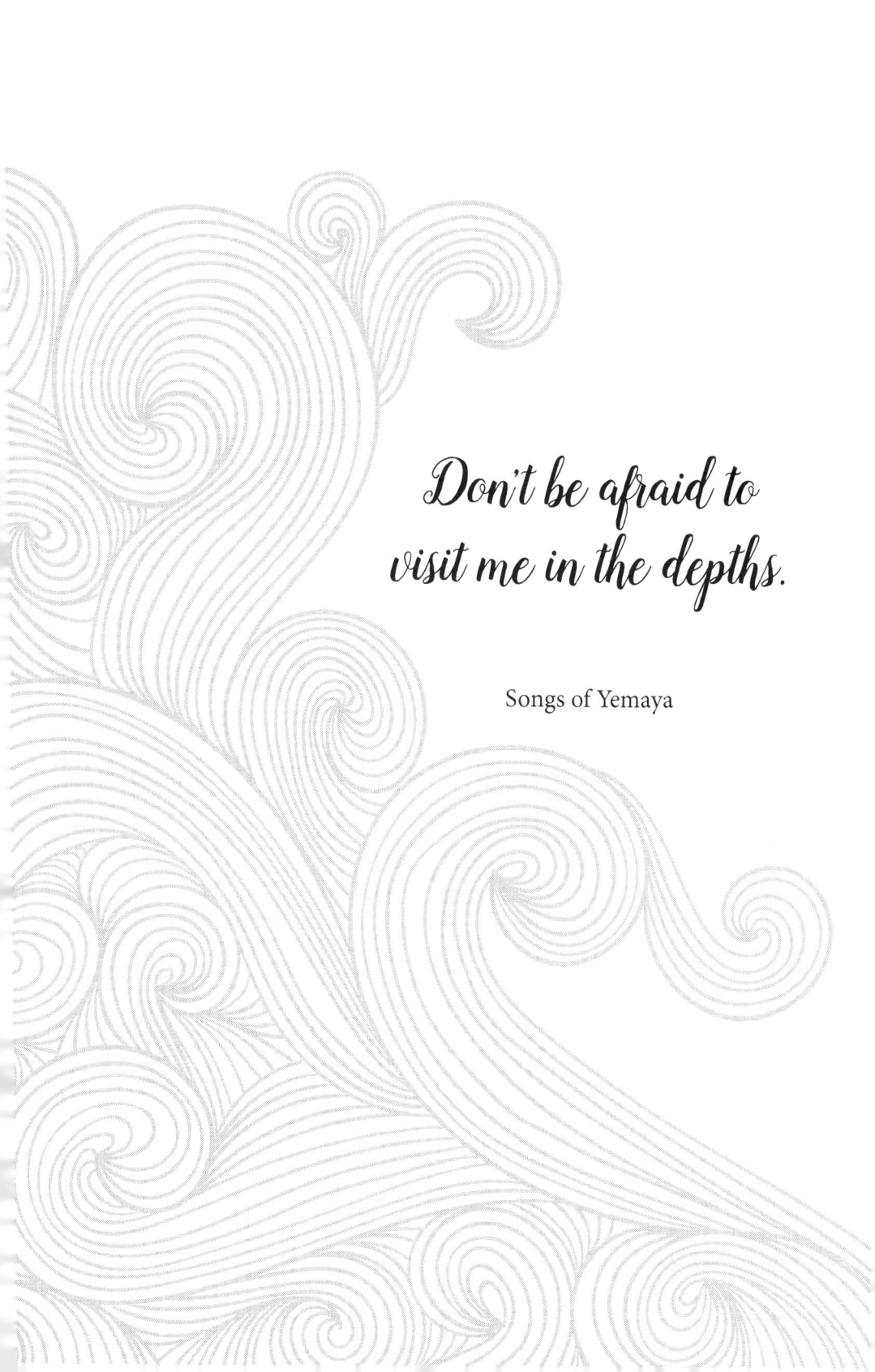

Songs of Yemaya

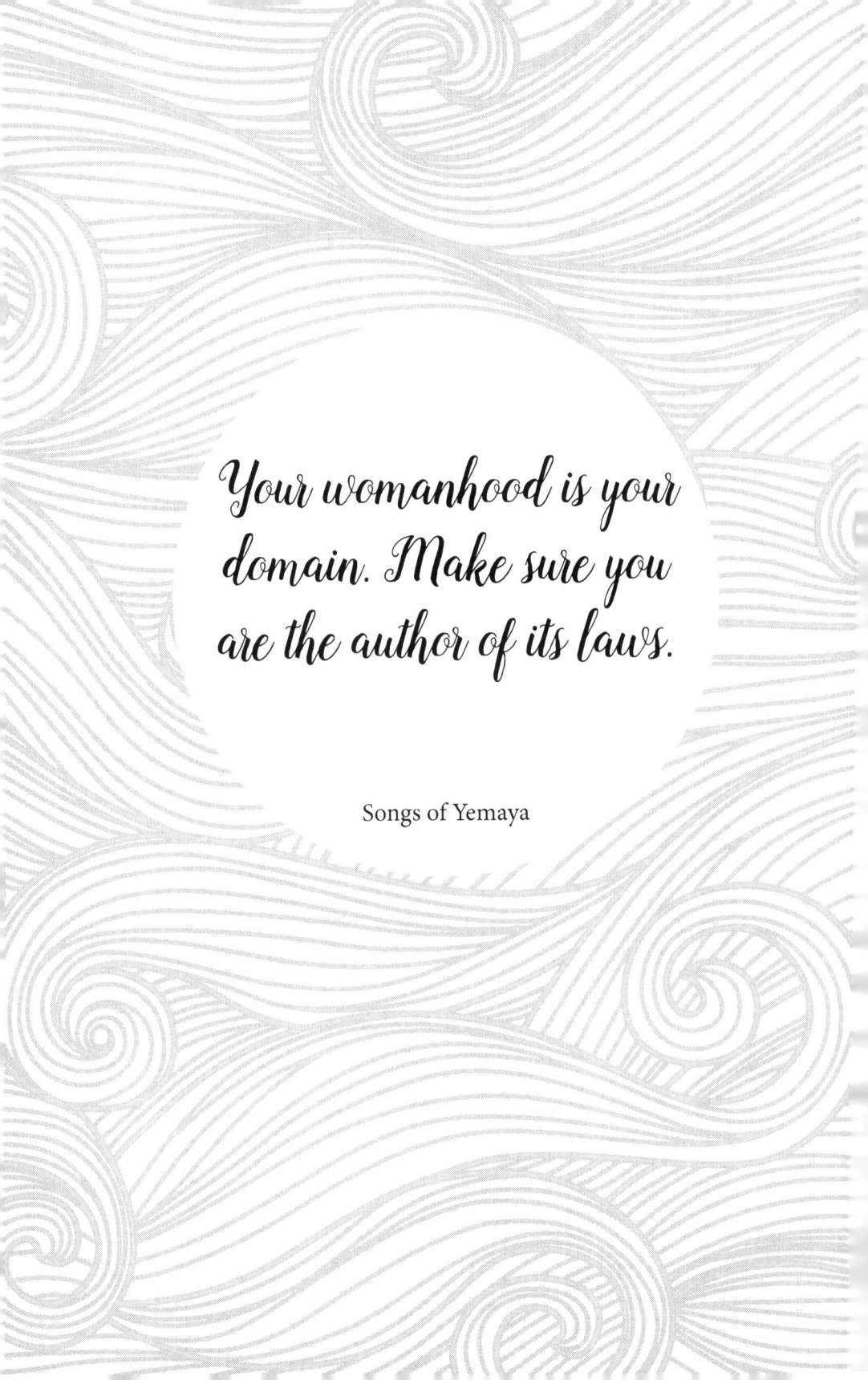

Your womanhood is your domain. Make sure you are the author of its laws.

Songs of Yemaya

Kehryse Vanessa Johnson

Kehryse Vanessa Johnson is a British Jamaican womanist and enemy of anti-blackness. Founder of EuroBlack women's empowerment group Code Ébène, she currently volunteers at the Black Cultural Archives in London and is in the middle of researching her first novel. For personal reasons, she plans to rush into neither marriage nor motherhood.

> 'Every woman is a rebel,
> and usually in wild revolt against herself.'
> – Oscar Wilde

RENÉE IN WILD REVOLT

And they never see me coming. And they can't work out my secret. And me not being as doll-faced as my lifestyle would imply makes them underestimate the truth, the magic. And my thighs aren't slim, and my hair is like fluff, and my breasts are too big, sitting lazily on my stomach as if they ballooned and one day popped. And I don't smile very much. And I say very little. And in this way, I can take stuff without a struggle, without anyone really noticing me or my movements, only that their things are gone.

And here I am, my back arched against the wall, Miguel rocking between my thighs. And the people dance beyond this wall—order drinks, talk shit, think they're having fun. And some are aware that we've slipped away. And they're aware that we're having more fun, real fun, and it's faster than them, and it's what they're all there for but too scared or ashamed or institutionalized to admit. And they sip their *Caipirinhas*. And they swipe the perpetual Tinder right. And they wish they could do this too but daren't step out into the night. And this is another of my nights.

And Miguel is close. And I claw at his hair. And he breathes hot on my skin. And I bite his neck. And he is probing. And we battle in angles. And he jerks forward, and he's pushing through, and I swell. And he trickles down my left leg and into my kitten heel. And I open my eyes. And he smiles greedily. And I laugh. And he laughs. And he doesn't realize that I'm laughing at him.

And he says: Did you come?

And I say: Yes. And now I'll go.

And all the girls from work, they know about my notches. And whilst they giggle with me, and I tell them stories, and they nod all sparkly-eyed—they never invite me to their weddings or birthday nights out or dinner nights in. And they don't realize that I have a plan. And they don't know that it is partly because of them, for them. And they continue to keep me at arm's length. And in this way, they feel safe. And they are in sync with the men without even realizing it. And that pisses me off. And I want so badly for them to know that I wouldn't steal their husbands. And I wouldn't roll around on their beds. And I wouldn't break up their happy homes: except to prove to them that it can be done. And that's a real reason, a good reason. And then they'd know that their men were no different. And that their marriages were no exception to the rules. And that makes it make sense. And it's all okay.

And here I am wearing one of *those* skirts to work. And I'm standing at the copier. And all eyes are on my body even though it's completely covered up. And it isn't my clothes or their colors that make others want to know what's beneath—but the way I walk from a room. And disappear in photos taken without the flash. And leave things unsaid, unfinished, unexplained. And the meeting is only minutes away now. And Ross is going to introduce me as the new team leader. And the girls will scowl. And the guys will nod once. And they'll think they understand why I'm suddenly their new boss. And they'll be absolutely wrong—I was on my knees in Ross's office last week because I wanted to be. And that's the truth. And I would tell them so if they had guts enough to ask. And not just fold their arms. And toss their 1A hair. And whisper like they were still in school.

And Ross finishes by saying: Congratulations and welcome!

And there is scattered applause.

And I say thank you. And they think I'm talking to them. And I'm not.

And this is all about guts. And I enjoy sex. And that makes this a test of the best guts and the best sex. And really, I'm on the search for that though it seems unattainable. And I want to know what's on offer. And in a way, this is proof in itself, this is the big reveal. And I don't wish to excuse any woman. And nor do I need to. And there's no such thing as going too far.

And here I am locked in my mother's bathroom hoisted up onto the sink. And Deon is breathing down my neck, wheezing like a little girl. And I want him to push harder, push faster, push deeper, but he says it's too soft, sweet, small. And this really only means that he's a one-minute man. And that he has to think about his Grandmother having a bath to prevent from the release after fifty-four seconds. And I squeeze his buttocks roughly; digging my nails right in. And I want him to return that grip, its divine pressure, make me bite my tongue down onto my lip. And fight to keep myself from growling. And he doesn't, no he doesn't, the selfish ass—he throws his head back. And breathes deep, eyes closed, sweat forming.

And I'm aware that he's not quite enough. And not quiet enough. And that if he doesn't shut up, we'll alert my family downstairs. And the exhilaration, all headiness will end abruptly with four sharp bangs on this door. And we'll be thrown out. And we won't get the fancy sit-down dinner. And my mother will be too ashamed and embarrassed to ever address it again. And she'll turn her eyes to the ground when she sees me in the street and hurry right past. And I can't stand her, but that's not something I want to see happen.

And the moment Deon's body locks, I shove him away. And he leans against the shower door with shaky shoulders and a bobbing head. And he looks beautiful, powerless, like if I was to poke him one-fingered, he would topple down into the tub. And I shake my head with a smirk—enjoying the fact that he believes I brought him here to meet my mother, when I actually did it to irritate her. And stir my ridiculous relatives with their warnings about biological clocks and single black female syndrome. And—most importantly of all—to fuck me on my mother's sink where she washes her face with carrot soap.

And Deon zips his weakest link away, whispering: You ready to go down?

And I tidy myself up, spit the words: You go first.

And he thinks I mean downstairs. And I really mean to hell.

And it's at a similarly relentless family gathering that my sister Sherine introduces us all to Antonio DePalma. And she announces that they're engaged to be married. And that this supposedly perfect day will take place next summer. And the man I've invited, whose name escapes me, squeezes my hand. And I twist it out of his grasp, right there, I bend his romance. And I turn to look at Antonio as Sherine's still speaking. And he's this dangerously hot Italian with a box-shaped head and large hands. And he wears a very nice suit, blinking thoughtfully through heavy lashes. And he greets everybody, in turn, bending to kiss both my mother's dusted cheeks. And there's a big whoop of excitement from my husky aunties. And I feel disappointed. And over dinner, as they chatter excitedly, I nibble on my too-chewy mutton, and I think about Sherine: the paler, delicate, and scented version of me. And how I've always tried to steer her in the right direction. And that it's a shame she's come to this.

And as the weeks pass I watch her, seeing into her, just like I always did as we were growing up. And yes, she's happy and alert and alive right now, but this is the very reason I must intervene. And let her down gently. And show her the truths of a woman's education. And stop her from turning into our hopeless mother, who wears the remnants of my father's desertion on her pupils everyday. And has done so since that very first morning. And it's a time, a day, a moment that I'll never forget; when events were not just reruns like they are now. And we woke up and it was blindingly sunny, and he had disappeared. And mother dashed out into the street in a headscarf, no shoes on, her head twisting from left to right. And he'd taken our money. And I first got my period. And no one was there to tell me why I just kept on bleeding. And I had to make myself understand.

And here I am, my face on fire after Sherine's steely slap to my cheek. And deafened momentarily, my head snaps forward again, the sound of her guttural howls returning slowly. And I can see now that she's hurt her hand. And yet the pain in her wrist, though sharp, is probably a welcome distraction from the waves of grief that inevitably come with knowing. And her nose is running, and her weave is frayed, and her eyes are like two black olives, swollen and shiny against her skin. And I feel saddened for her, I do, I feel grainy, hollow, ripped—as if it were me all over again. And I hate to be the bearer of bad news. And I hate to witness it sink in, sink in for my Sherine of all women, but I know that my timing is the best it could have been. And truth always hits hard, like a head-on collision; it smashes everything up.

And now they're holding her back, and she's kicking with all her might to reach me, and she's crying out that I'm a dirty whore. And though I love her most severely I resent what she's saying. And I want to correct her but don't. And whilst she's picking up objects and flinging them in my direction and blubbering all over her layered white dress, I think about those loaded words. And I'm safe in the knowledge that I am not one of those, that I had real reasons, good reasons. And that my sex with Antonio wasn't lewd. And it wasn't unlawful. And it wasn't anything, except what I wanted it to be; which is educational.

And Sherine's determined to torture herself. And so, I give in, I answer her questions: tell her where we had sex, exactly how many times, and in what variations. And I want her to remember where she was at those times, what she was doing, who she was with whilst all the while being lied to. And in this way, she'll have a visual recollection, never forget the lesson she's learnt here, never be so damned foolish again. And she listens and listens now until she is tired, cracked, buckling. And I think it's over….

And with incredible venom, she roars: You fucking ain't my fucking sister!

And I answer: Yes, you're right.

And the last thing I feel is guilty, of course, I don't, I'm not—because I did nothing wrong. And I made a point of not having an orgasm with Antonio DePalma. And I made a point of not enjoying it. And I pictured Sherine's face every second that he was inside me. And I did it, all of it, to save her. And she's been lucky to have me. And she doesn't yet realize. And no, I don't mean as her sister, no, because I'm much more than that to her now: I'm her savior. And instead of trying to harm me it would have been better if she had identified the real villain, the true stealer of her dreams, as I did back when I was one of those drowning women. And Cameron Wight was my only reason for being. And our relationship was the ocean. And I ate, slept, drank him until that coffee-colored woman, the parting of her legs, the awakening of my core and absolute truths.

And when I was ready I telephoned that woman. And I asked for her name. And she was surprised at the low level of my voice, the controlled tone with which I addressed her. And she answered my questions, painted them with colors that I still see. And she told me who she was.

And I said thank you.

And I meant to thank you for everything.

And my name is Renée. And it's been a pleasure to meet you.

Lise-May Arnal

Lise-May Arnal, who now resides in Europe, studied philosophy and literature before undertaking a career in disease prevention. An interest in journalism and photography was also embraced simultaneously and was developed mostly in the black press—Nommo, Ariztos, African Affairs, Africulture. Lise-May worked as a radio DJ (1991-1998: WKCR, KCSB), mostly to familiarize auditors with African music, issues in the black community, and reggae artists, which at the time was not widespread. She has published three books: *Broke in L.A., Third World USA,* and *The Secret of the Statue.*

STRENGTH OF SONGS

We are the mothers, the lovers,
Bread-winners, breast-feeders…
We are the woe-men of his dreams;
The sanctified whores, and venerated bitches

of his fearful fantasies
Paralyzed

By our self-enmity
Our soft struggles
And superfluous
lingerie

Centuries linger by
And wonder why
We led a dead end,
Pseudo-liberation
as we are stuck
impotently sexy

with beseeched moans
— mourners of our dreams —

There soars, within
The hope-beached breast
of yours, a song of strength;
The rebellious demands
of amorous morrows
Awaiting

your willful move
— Body and Mind —

Melissa Dunmore

Melissa Dunmore is a poet, published writer, and earnest connector. She is a desert islander with roots in rural Puerto Rico where she was born. She was raised in Brooklyn, New York, and transplanted to Phoenix, Arizona, area over a decade ago. Over the past five years, she has deftly expanded into one brave topic after another through spoken word performance. Her work exudes themes of Afro-Latina multicultural identity, bilingualism, and diaspora.

MEMORIES LIKE MAMMARIES

Memories
Like mammaries
I have grown
I own them
I have shown them
To men
Women
The walls of my private spaces
Other's faces
Delight in them
Discovery
Of me
The curves
The perks
The buoyancy
Of my memories
Like mammaries
That I own
I owe them
My pride
Stride
Silent smirks and wisdom
Which paint the walls
In filigree
Philanthropy
And graces
My private spaces.

Queen Ella Zuree

Queen Ella Zuree is a biomedical engineer who also writes poetry, short stories, and blogs. She currently resides in Phoenix, Arizona. She is a fun-loving, art-loving, single mother raising a 12-year-old girl and a two-month-old son.

SHATTERED

I want you to fix me but I'm afraid to give you my pieces.

Catherine Toppin

Catherine Toppin is a patent attorney and global team leader with General Electric in Norwalk, Connecticut. Catherine earned her B.S. in Electrical Engineering from Princeton University, and her J.D. from the University of Maryland. Catherine has been recognized for her volunteerism and professional leadership, most recently as a 2017 recipient of The Network Journal's 40 Under Forty Achievement Award. In her spare time, she enjoys speaking to students about education and career choices, playing the violin with the New Westchester Symphony Orchestra, exercising, and dancing salsa.

ERR ON THE SIDE OF OVER-CONFIDENCE

There are things in this life that get stapled to you. They are attached superficially enough, but come with definitive pain and often without your permission. 1993 was the first time I can remember being called ugly. I was twelve years old, and wasn't called ugly outright; rather, one of my girlfriends casually reported back to me that her then ninth-grade boyfriend had sniffed out a reckless, "She's not that ugly."

In a twisted game of telephone, my girlfriend passed that message along to me.

Ring-ring, pick-up, "You're ugly."

Message received.

I reasoned, thought through, and concluded that my girlfriend and her boyfriend had probably had multiple conversations concerning the status of my appearance. And even more clearly, I deduced that my girlfriend was likely the one who said that I was straight-up ugly, not the downgraded version her boyfriend felt the authority to declare and she the authority to report back.

Honey-girl-supposed-to-be-sista-child-friend had not defended me against such an assertion. I knew that she had been complicit if not the author of the words. My bloom had been on display without my knowledge, and the conclusion was that my type of bloom was not desirable, or at the least not desirable enough. The conclusion was painful and problematic for a young woman budding into brown, into body, into her legs, into the world. The joy in my friend's face when informing me of her boyfriend's declaration of "not-that-ugly" status was equally as perplexing as it was hurtful. *Honey-girl-sista-child-friend* had claimed her stake in determining who was blooming the right way, and our friendship would be secondary to the proclamation. I retreated in her betrayal.

Having grown up in a conservative, reserved, and strict Christian West Indian home in a majority black American middle-class suburban backdrop, there were certain conversations I had just not been privy to yet. I grew up in a large family, seven of us in total: mom, dad, two older brothers, a younger sister, and a younger brother. Making fun of each other and being made fun of was a part of the love and texture of my family life. Verbal roughhousing was the norm with a family so large, but until that day, I had the luxury of never contemplating being societally ugly nor dealing with the heinous social ramifications of that declaration in middle school until that day.

A few days later, bothered and having mulled over the "ugly" news, I mustered up enough courage to mention the situation to my petite Bajan mother, who for a brief moment in time stood eye to eye with me in stature. My mother's response was smooth and short, rising up like warm air from her mouth; her petite stature dressed in the color of fall suede was resolute and direct. She looked at me and asked, "Catherine, do you think you are ugly?"

And before I could indulge in a piteous response, she interjected with, "Whose opinion is more important, yours or theirs?" The questions were self-sufficient, unlike my esteem at the time. The questions were existential enough that they were meant to stand alone. She was efficient, and her petite frame had no more hot air to douse on the subject; and, whether intentional or not, the process of allowing me to come to my own conclusion was pivotal.

The simple logic of her question had long legs.

Legs that would eventually belong to a self-assured woman who would become five feet nine inches tall and an Ivy League educated engineer. Legs that would belong to a woman who would receive a scholarship to attend a tier one law school, become a lawyer at a Fortune 10 company, and receive professional performance evaluations as "erring on the side of overconfident" by white male colleagues and higher-ups as a place for improvement.

The audience of black women and black girls is wide, and so is the critique. The world says that black women and girls are "too much, not enough, too strong, not soft enough, oversexed, under desired, slightly above the animals." While these proclamations may be stapled to you by society, don't take them on as a permanent feature. Examine them, if you must, and then quickly rip out their superficial attachment to your identity.

Over the years I have been called many things, many of which are far worse than "not-that-ugly." From being called "gorilla" by the star player on my high school basketball team during practice, to "Amazon" by a law firm partner during a celebratory dinner in honor of me passing the bar, the world has uttered its ugly names.

Each time a word is used to define or judge us, we have the power to define its meaning, to determine our interpretation of its relative importance, to serve as the final judge of its truth, and to decide our response to it. In a world that utters its words against you, speak boldly the words that you yourself own. Believe the best about yourself, and then set out to live up to that belief through your actions. Living life in this world will surely give you a journey. Take it on!

Had I been a bit older, or a little more experienced, I may have realized that my childhood friend was dealing with her own notions of belonging in a world that denigrates black women freely and builds so reluctantly the worth of black girls. Maybe I would have realized that her boyfriend was also working with a paradigm that relegated me into some hierarchy that he was grappling to understand. My twelve-year-old self didn't understand those nuances and that my "not-that-ugly-moment" would one day become the "be-careful-not-to-err-on-the-side-of-overconfident" review!

To be overconfident in this world, black women, is a resistance. It is to be an island, and a revolution in its own right.

So breathe, love, revolt, be confident, and err in that way. And whenever you get the chance, tell another black or brown woman or girl just how beautiful she is.

TOO SOMETHING

Too… everything

No sir
I did not benefit from anyone's favor
For Caucasians found me too black or
Too ugly
And Africans too white,
Both uncannily
Too much of an uppity-negro

Men, too broke, too old, and un-docile
Women, too liberated and un-meek

No, m'am
The Earth did not open at my feet
And they have grown much tired
Of the easy contempt and the overloads of hatred

I have not used my looks
For I have worked pretty
Much
All my tedious life
And alone, too

And I deserve every bit of success I have ploughed into the soiled black woman's destiny
Of mine
And I deserve the love I've been yearning for
Way too long

Despite the whirling crowds of useless men
The parasites, the users or abusers, the neurotics, and sadistic individuals
That people this abused land

But is love—for an African woman—too much to ask for?
For love is my thing

Too something—
worth everything.

Christiana Harrell

Christiana Harrell, originally from New Orleans, started writing at a young age. She started as a blogger sharing her thoughts on love and relationships. In 2009, Christiana published her first book, a short story collection entitled *GIRL*. She debuted her first full-length novel, *The D in Drama*, in 2012. Her latest accomplishment came a year later when her title, *Cream*, was nominated for a Lambda Literary award. To date, Christiana has eleven titles: three short story collections, two poetry books, three novellas, and three stand-alone novels. She's still counting the number of stories she has yet to tell.

LIKE COFFEE

I had an identity before either of my parents even thought about me. When God knew that I'd be a woman, the world already pegged me strong and angry. My strength would come from watching my mother take care of my sister, and I alone and my anger would stem from that same place. I'd grow as the statistic of so many other black boys and girls. The only difference is my daddy issues would be the source of my problem for the rest of my life. It would be the crown I wore on my head and the cape on my back. If you didn't have a daddy, then you didn't have anyone to tell you that you were beautiful. If you didn't have a daddy, then you were never taught how a man should treat you. If you didn't have a daddy, you were bound to be promiscuous because every boy that called you pretty gave you the love that daddy never gave you and you *had* to give it back.

Your sex was your love.

I had to learn on my own that everyone was wrong, because even though I didn't have a daddy, I had a mother. I had a grandmother. I had a great-grandmother. Black ones. Ones who, without knowing, would tell us how "niggas ain't shit." We'd get to watch as men treated our home like a revolving door during my mother's own quest for love. Watching my mother in tears more than once was enough to teach me what I deserved or thought I deserved. After all, we never had the conversation. My great-grandmother would give me what I thought was sound advice, saying, "As long as you have a pussy, you should never be broke."

Not once had I been told about the raping of black women or the disgusting displays of our bodies. Not once had I been told that with that advice, I had a choice. Nobody taught me about the power I possessed.

My mother was young, but she reminded us daily of the beauty within us as well as on the outside, silently. I remember dancing around the living room one day in a gown that was two sizes too small. I was sixteen and developing more than anybody my age. My sister stood next to me dancing, too. Our mother shook her head, blurting out that she wished she could just lock us away in the basement and throw away the key. She warned us then about the dangers of our curves. She knew about the slight praise and degradation that we, as two black girls, would face outside the safety of the home she built for us. The home where we could be ourselves.

Even with her subtle warning, I lived in my own world. Too young to realize that catcalling was not flattery but harassment, I'd giggle my way up a street from a store; because in my mind, I should feel lucky to even get the attention of a boy. I had to start early if I wanted a husband, right? Black men weren't checking for black women, right? We were the least sought after and most unlikely to get married, right? Right. I remember feeling overwhelmingly overjoyed when a boy told me I was pretty for a black girl. I didn't see the problem in his "compliment." I just knew that if he saw beauty in me at my level of blackness, I had to be something.

Although my mom did all she could to keep me and my sister from making the same mistakes she had made, she forgot to block the conditioning that taught us how to need a man and why. I read books and watched movies that kept me in that loop of black women who were strong but not too strong, black but not too black, and definitely not too proud. I learned to be comfortable with processed hair because it was the only acceptable way to wear it. I wore revealing clothing and flashy jewelry. I was loud and always needed to be seen. Weaves were of the devil for a while, then they became life. Only people who smoked weed wore dreads. Freaks were in the sheets and ladies were in the streets—yeah, right. Anything too revealing could get you raped. Anything too revealing meant you were asking for it. There seemed to be an unwritten handbook on femininity and blackness that I had to follow strictly or be cast out. I went with the wind of every trend, unable to stand out and sit on my throne.

I followed these rules for years, knowing my role as a brown girl and my place on the privilege totem pole. I accepted that I wasn't that special. My hair was "nappy" and my skin wasn't light enough. My ass was too big, and so were my lips and nose. All the love I thought I had dwindled the moment I started to compete and compare.

There were several hands in my mental and spiritual downfall. Since I was already weak, it was nothing to be happy with someone who had dated light-skinned women all their lives then made me feel lucky because for once they tried something different with me on their arm. All the while reminding me that I was in fact still not what they really wanted. I was just pretty, and pretty wasn't enough without the "right" complexion.

Something had to give.

I don't remember the exact moment I found myself, but I remember the people who showed me a better way. I always thought it would be a man, because for some reason I still needed the validation of my father. Of course, it has not and will not happen. Finally, I'm okay with that. It was black women who would come to my rescue.

When you are asked, "Do you know who you are?", you have to stop for a second and evaluate before you answer. That's what happened to me. I had no idea who I was other than a clone of what society wanted me to be. Somewhere between magazines and television, I'd lost my mirror. I'd forgotten that I had my mother's eyes and teeth. I'd forgotten that I had my father's nose and feet. Things inherited from my ancestors over centuries of reproduction. The long lines of people who made it possible for me to exist and be proud.

One day, my mother and father would not be here, and all they'd have left is who they created: me. I'd have to represent them in power and positivity. I'd have to be everything they were not. It was a slow and hard transition as I began to let go of the things that started me on a dreaded journey.

The first thing that started to break were my ideas of religion. The images of a white Jesus and the teachings of oppression had to go. I had found my voice, and I had questions.

Questions that would make a pastor stutter if he didn't have enough time to think of a new lie. My vocabulary began to change as I discovered books that told me about patriarchy and propaganda—things that were put into place to keep me feeling that I was less than what I actually was, a QUEEN.

In April 2011, the physical changes began. I started with my hair, cutting out the damage from processing it for over twenty-four years. With every strand came a level of liberation that I had not experienced before.

I felt free.

That same week, I brushed my waves and dressed to kill for a night out on the town with my sister, who was celebrating her birthday. As we partied on New Orleans' popular Bourbon Street, my confidence elevated as both men and women rubbed their hands across my bald head and did all they could to get my attention. I was standing in the world as myself for the first time in my life—no make-up, no false nails, and no weave down my back. It was just me, my curves, and my black skin.

I was hungry for more of the inner peace that I began to feel. I found it in my soul, in silence, in darkness, in love and light. I found it by surrounding myself with like-minded people who loved life and appreciated the little things. I found it in the unlearning of my conditionings. I was awake.

There were and still are bits of misery inside of me, because now my chaos comes from watching other black women and men who have not made the discovery of self. My own mother is still that same woman who thinks she consumes the right type of pride. As bad as it may sound, I'm happy to no longer be her, but to be a better version.

I await the day that I will have a daughter to place on a pedestal, to be able to break the chains of self-hatred that I had to break for myself. She will first be a little black princess, then a queen on a throne that was rightfully hers from birth.

Cherise Charleswell

Cherise Charleswell is an Afro-Caribbean-Latina who is an intersectional and transnational feminist and reluctant "academic." She is an anthropologist, womanist, author/writer, and public health researcher/practitioner who serves as the Chair of Women's Issues for The Hampton Institute. Cherise is a segment producer and co-host on Feminist Magazine KPFK 90.7FM on the Pacifica Radio Network, and a globe-trotter. Her work has appeared in publications as diverse as: *For Harriet, Black Women Unchecked, Zocalo The Public Square, Truth Out, Rewind & Come Again,* and in various academic/professional journals. She is the co-editor of *Walking in the Feminine: A Stepping Into Our Shoes Anthology.* She is an activist who makes it a point to constantly call out, push back, and actively address misogynoir.

THERE IS NO GAP

I can shop for hours, trying on shoes and clothes, and ignoring or not noticing hunger pains. However, grocery shopping is a task I dread. I grab my shopping list and reusable cloth bags, and throw them into the cart, which I navigate and push through the meandering aisles of grocery markets, like a Nascar driver. The entire trip is time-consuming, and I cannot stand it when other shoppers peek into my cart and begin to take inventory. That is when the comments begin, "Well, you certainly eat healthy," along with the, "So, is that how you maintain THAT body?" and the, "No meat? Yet ALL of that booty," and so on. Somehow the simple act of purchasing food draws attention to my body.

I try to eat healthy in hopes of maintaining my body. I, like all other women, have an image of what my body "should" look like. And that image is so powerful that any extra pounds, noticeable loss of muscle definition, or signs of cellulite quickly change my mood and render me temporarily depressed, or frustrated. During my menstrual "blood-letting" days, I prefer to wear loose and stretchy fabrics because anything else would reveal an abdominal area that is bloated, not flat and taut.

I'm sure it sounds like I may be a closeted anorexic or bulimic, but that is not the case. My body has been referred to as thick, shapely, and curvaceous. I am just about 5'11, wear a US size 8 dress, a 36C bra (I am refusing to get re-measured and possibly placed in a D cup), and my curvy thighs touch. There is NO gap, and I actually love my body for the most part. As long as I can control it, maintain it, and mold it into my desired image, where I can remain thick and healthy: flat abs, small waist, rounded hips, perky and ample breasts, shapely derrière, with thunderous thighs that have No gap.

I watch and monitor my body, even "listening" to the way it feels, to ensure that I do not cross the line into obesity and suffer the subsequent chronic diseases. As a public health specialist, I am most interested in health, and not just the aesthetics: my ideal body type. However, I would not be forthcoming if I did not admit that I am not greatly concerned with the image I see in the mirror's reflection. If I did not admit that I stand nude and completely vulnerable in front of that mirror, evaluating my body weekly. Looking to see what may have changed and what needs to be "fixed" through dietary changes along with increased exercise and physical activity.

I am by no means a calorie counter, and for the most part, I eat what I most desire and try to make up for it by ensuring that the majority of my diet includes healthier options, such as fruits, vegetables, and complex carbohydrates. My favorite breakfast is a large bowl of steel cut oats, and if you throw in a few raisins, even better! Also, when I am ready, I allow myself to enjoy a few slices of pizza, apple pie, or even a glazed cinnamon donut. I give in and indulge on occasion.

The truth: I can hike, weight train, jog, dance, do a cardio circuit workout, squats, jumping jacks, side bends, and sit-ups; and my thighs will only grow stronger, bigger, thicker, broader, and more muscular. They will never be thin. They will never be fragile. There is NO gap. I was once told that my thighs looked like they could crush an apple and produce apple juice while performing the dreaded chore of grocery shopping, and I accept that. While the mainstream media and fashion magazines promote angular bodies that at times resemble prepubescent boyhood or Eurocentric ideals of beauty that explicitly exclude my front-to-back curvaceous body, I don't shrink. The type of body that I have, I accept and celebrate. There is NO gap between the thighs, and I am just fine with that.

Radhiyah Ayobami

Radhiyah Ayobami, Brooklyn-born by way of the South, tells stories of black womanhood, motherhood and folks in invisible spaces. She believes the word has the power to shift consciousness. She writes and workshops with pregnant teens, inmates and elders, and is an Africana Studies graduate of Brooklyn College and MFA prose student at Mills College in Oakland, California. She is working on a collection of nonfiction essays and the trees give her poems.

UNDER THE VEIL

women at the masjid say- mashallah!
girls in class say- is you religious or something?
employers say- we don't allow headgear.
owners of the bodegas say- you are not dead like the rest of your people.
christians say- turn aside false gods.
rastas say- burn the pope!
poets say- i thought you didn't drink.
your special friend says- why you don't take that off & wear a tight skirt?
men on the corner say- so you can't have no man?
women handing out beauty salon cards say- we twist dreadlocs!
the incense man says- support black business goddamit.
airport staff- step to the side, please.
old aunties say- you used to be right nice-looking.
five percenters say- peace earth.
yoga teachers say- remove all outer coverings.
the weed man says- i put a little something on it because i know you righteous.
the veil says:
- don't go to that gathering. stay home.
- that's enough chocolate. have an apple.
- someone was fighting here. say a prayer.
- eat red clover buds.
- you must leave that house. i will show you where to go.
- read your womb poem tomorrow.
- make potato soup for your mother.
- see those roses by the park bench. pick them for the altar
  & you will receive your request.
- peaches!
- put your hand on his shoulder but tell him no. he will still respect you.
- take the class. it will be useful later on.
- here comes billy goats gruff. smile at her & she won't complain.
- the sister is having a baby. tell her all will be well.
- go to the fire.
- listen. be quiet. this is what to do.

I got sisters in different area codes.

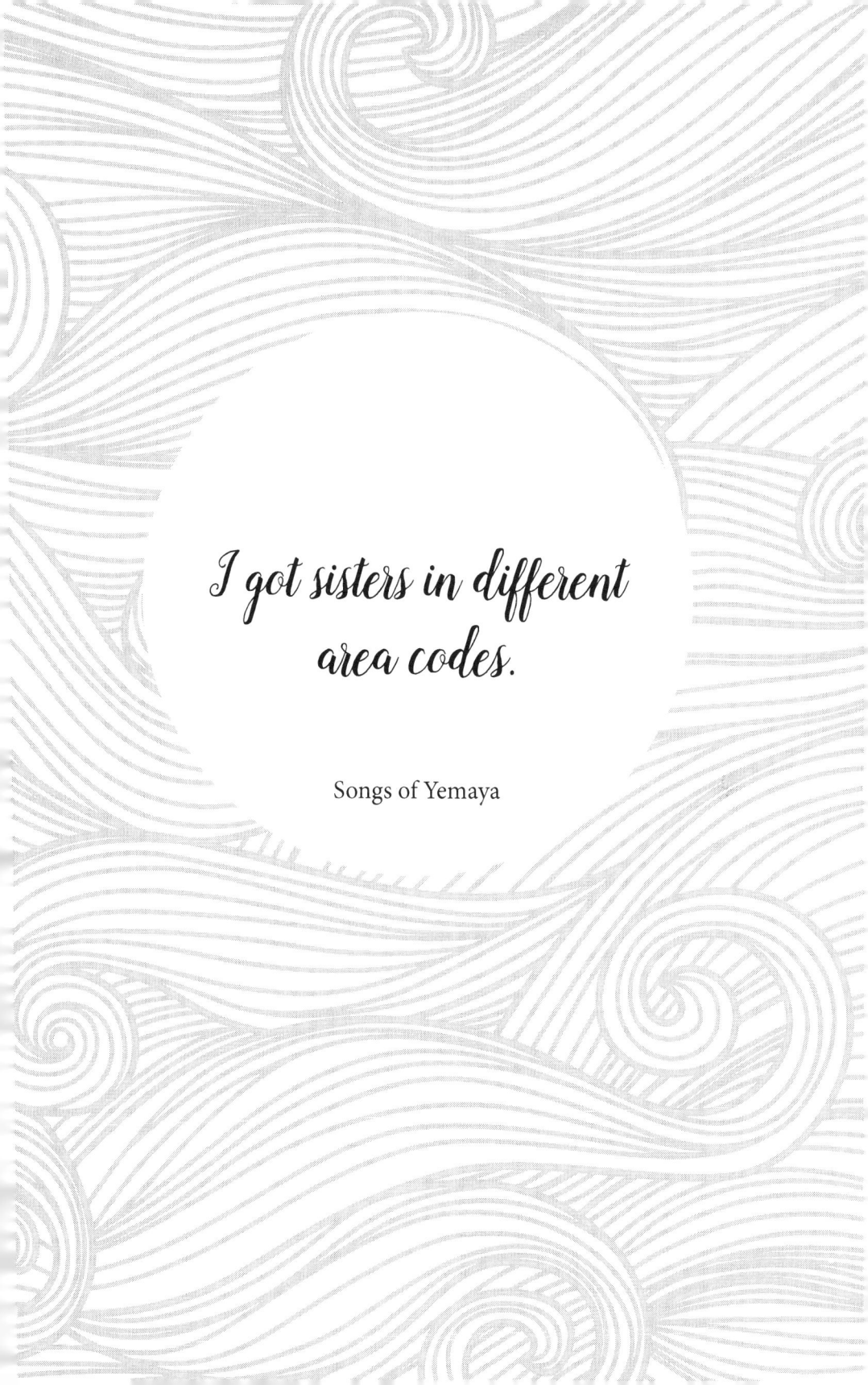

Songs of Yemaya

MANIFESTO

recently, i heard a story that made me very happy. in fact, it actually made me feel joy. it was a story about a close sista-friend of mine. i have known her for about ten years. we met when our children went to the same cultural school (our friendship has outlived the school as well). i was in my early 20s; she was about 30. i was transitioning into the cultural world, growing locs, and exploring different traditions. she had already been married to a community leader, and she eased me into her circle and her way of life. she introduced me to roots reggae dances and was the first person i met who blessed herb before smoking it. she took me to african spiritual events and explained the protocol; how to cleanse before entering, when to stand and when to kneel, how to give an offering and receive a blessing. wherever we went, folks cracked into wide smiles as soon as she was on the scene. she was forever being waved at across a crowded room, greeting other smiling people, and being enveloped by hugs.

as the years progressed, we went through the same initiations, starved through the same fasts, partied at the same events in long skirts and headwraps on a wednesday night, and were late getting our kids to school in the morning. we piled our children and some other folks' children in a half-working car and drove to all-night drum circles where they fell asleep under trees as we meditated by the fire. we survived on the same small handful of greens in a foreign country when it had rained too much and everybody was hungry, and when the sun came out we all washed up outside in broad daylight, everything jiggling, breasts that had nursed babies, waistbeads, and our locs heavy with water from the sea.

and then came the curves of life. we went to city offices and through housing systems, patching together the help we needed to move forward. we created resumes and got jobs that paid on the books and took out taxes. we transitioned out of our small communities and found that wearing extra long skirts and yards of cloth around our shoulders was sometimes not practical when working with small children or in various other settings. she was first to cut her locs and put on pants, and one day she came walking around the corner on fulton street with no headwrap, no multi-colored skirt swishing her ankles, and no scent of sacred oil, and i walked right by her. she had a short afro, creased pants, and a folder full of resumes, and something about the outfit reminded me of the colorful birds i saw languishing in cages at the zoo. months later, when my son and i lived in a building that awakened us with five am fire alarms, she wrote me a letter that helped me transition out of that place and into an apartment where my porch was the entire roof and i could sit and watch the sky.

and then we went into the next decade of our lives, and i listened to her laugh become a little less loud as she watched friends and family marry and waltz across the dance floor in each other's arms as she raised her children and drove to the occasional roots dance on her own. we began to talk about the beliefs and traditions that kept us bound to the idea of being honorable women. elders told us that we shouldn't be out past nine o'clock. imams said we should be in by maghrib. at the drumming ceremonies, we couldn't uncover our hair (even though it was hot by the fire, and the breeze through our locs would have been the greatest blessing). in almost every tradition, we were lectured against smoking herb, and told to have husbands instead of lovers, so we wouldn't damage our spirits. so me and my sista-friend began to have conversations. we began to wonder, under the skirts and scarves and rules and admonishments, where we could find the seed of joy. our communities and traditions had sustained and nurtured us, but now we were in a new cycle of life, and it was time for change. we talked and argued with each other, we fasted and went to steam baths and spiritual events and prayed and sat with our own thoughts. and then, we moved.

she broke the no lovers rule first, and invited me over for tea so we could talk about it, and it was a conversation that lasted all night. it was winter when she broke that rule, and it was summer when i broke it, and i ended up writing a lot of poems. and we discovered some things. we discovered that another human being, particularly a partner, fixing a meal that you like or washing your hair or giving you advice on a complicated problem late at night even though they were tired, or rubbing your foot deep enough to ease out the soreness of the day was just as holy as a drum ceremony or lighting an incense stick or the pouring of water—and maybe, even more holy than that. we discovered that the best rules to follow were the ones that brought our spirits balance and joy.

and after awhile, my sista-friend stayed in pants. she never went back into daily headwraps and long skirts—although she would wear them occasionally for events or if she felt like it. i stayed in long skirts and wraps because my womanself loved them, but sometimes wore jeans if i wanted to, and we never gave up dancing or late nights or wine or bud. we still prayed and chanted and burned and poured sacred water—but we carried no flags but our own.

and then today she called me, ashamed, because she was out on a date with a man that made her heart glow, and they had a little taste of wine and a little smoke, and they went to a roots party, and she ran into folks she knew, and there she was in a short skirt and a wild afro, kinda high, kinda drunk, with a strange and non-cultural man, and all the women were in there with headwraps up to the ceiling and skirts down to the floor. well, i fell out. i laughed and laughed. because at the age and stage that we're in now, does it really matter? we are far enough into this journey that we know most things are between us and the creator. when i was living in the five am fire alarm place, i was plagued with headaches so bad that i walked around with tylenol tucked into every pocket, every bag, and even under my headwrap for emergencies. and her letter helped me get into a house where the birds would come sing at the windows in the mornings when the sky was still pink, and i didn't have a bottle of tylenol in that whole house. and some of those women in those skirts would never do that for anyone else—some of them were devils. i know, because i wear long skirts and i'm a devil when i wanna be too.

and i wish my sista-friend a hundred dances in a hundred short skirts, if that's what feeds her soul. and for the rest of us, i wish us permission to be unbound to whatever it is that binds us. sometimes i look at my life—i'm in an expensive grad school but got no money. i'm an older black woman in an mfa program, which is generally made up of students who are young, male, and white. i'm fat, but i do african dance and yoga, and i love it, even when i'm the biggest person in the class, which is often. i moved across the country with a teenager, which everyone says is the worst time to move a child, and now he's closer to the honor roll than he's ever been. i've made a lot of mistakes, but my son and i have also had some great adventures. life has been our guide, our teacher, and our protector. and as shaky as my progress is, i'm continuing on my journey to be fully unbound, fully engaged in the process of life instead of watching it drift by, and fully committed to living with joy.

i give myself permission to:

honor my inner guidance
create my own family makeup
not explain or apologize for my choices
not explain, excuse, or defend my size, culture, or style of dress
treat my body kindly no matter what it looks like
tell my truth even when it's uncomfortable
tell the stories of my ancestors
pursue all my passions
ask for and accept compensation for my talents
not be afraid or ashamed of mistakes
choose teachers by spirit and not external affiliations
walk away when i need to
humble myself only to the elements: water, sun, trees, land & sky

Juanita Cox

Juanita Cox was born in Nigeria and lived there before being sent to boarding school in Cumbria, England at the age of 10 by her Ghanaian mother and English father. She moved to London in 1990 and worked as a personal assistant before getting a B.A. in Caribbean Studies and Mass Communications at London Metropolitan University. She moved with her husband to the interior of Guyana after completing a Ph.D. at the University of Birmingham in 2013 while working on the novels of the pioneering author, Edgar Mittelholzer. In 2015, she returned to London where she currently resides. Her first poem, *We Were Born on a Sunday*, falls under the theme of diasporic consciousness and explores identity through her matrilineal line. The second poem, *Mami Wata Cradles*, is an elegy that touches on the themes of diasporic displacement, motherhood, loss, and faith in Yemanja.

WE WERE BORN ON A SUNDAY

1. [SALTPOND, GHANA: 1681]

My name is Eresi Mebrabrabio
I'm tall like palm wine tree
My husband calls me Odo
Yes, Odo, for he loves me like the smooth
Arabic coffee I warm for him at break of day
But few know me.
I am Mami Wata:
I hide my wares in Egyaa number two,
I sell them in Kormantse,
I come home with beads.

2. [JOS, NIGERIA: 1979]

Sister Esi Panyin; now she is a marvel to behold
Hair like crown of Frangipani tree; body
Tall like Araba; skin smooth like
Clay, Bukuru laterite; and eyes,
Eyes wide like Bush-Baby.
Many fear the lash of her tongue,
Bulala tongue that fells Baobab tree
Faster than a Kwado-frog catches flies.
But her smile, when it comes, is the cool, cool of
Rain after a season of punishing dry.

3. [LONDON, ENGLAND: 2000]

Eresi, I wanted to have your name
But mother said no,
I wanted to carry your crying mark
But mother said no,
Sister Panyin did not care. She drank
Our loss and she laughed: "Let's go to the
Niger Bend and bury bare feet in the dust!"
My name is Esi Kakraba and
That is how it was.

BLACK SHE

My Black Daddy
his family didn't deem me Black enough
I - dirty blood - "spic" - mutt, mulatto
as if Black leaks from a well the only way to be
Black was to be their Black
which was not all that Black
at all more cafe au lait than
espresso mix of Gullah, White & Indian Black
Black descended
from slaves Black on land
for centuries and generations of commingling Black
Why was I their problem?
caramel colored cute and eager
never to identify fully as
Black coming up knowing
Latina - feeling it in the seams of abuela's rugs
the smells of her kitchen
rat tat tat of her radiator
musky smell of dish towels
abuelo's orange rinds hanging from the ceiling fans
swaying like a song
reused tea bags soup
when I was sick driven delivery
transportation whistling on
the stairs echo like a haunt
Sacred Heart everywhere
lenguaje - traditional superstition
What was wrong?

half of me missing yet nothing missing
gas tank full hand cramp
My Black Daddy from whom I
get my bushy eyebrows my
gapped two front teeth before
braces erased resemblance
correspondence long curly lashes
the mocha in my skin
coarse hair still there
underneath I am
your Black Child
    Black Daughter
    Black Girl
    Black Curls
    Black World
double consciousness all or nothing
nothing sometimes it is dark
there to know I am Black
- Black on both sides -
Tainos mixing genetic juices with Africans
Spaniards making wastelands
abuela's mother's hair
abuela's Black brother
skin sprawling like coattails
magnificent strong and I just
want to be Black because of
My Black Daddy
who doesn't call doesn't remember at all

how do you deny your Black Child Black Daughter
Black Girl Black World leave
her alone in a Black World like
Bat Girl fighting crimes forged
in her own bloodline - severed -
cast aside like a waistband
I've gone down around
spread out and collapsing
Black Star
Black Hole
Black Gold
Black Dynasty
Who will my children be?
They will be Black
Black like me
Black like My Black Daddy
not near not far I carry you
in my bloodline
   It is all mine
No one can take it from me
You can't take it back your
Black Body
Black Genes
Black Attack
Black Ballsack
Black Inseams
Black Dreams
I say they are mine
Black like every time I open my eyes
Black like every time I open my mind

   I sing you
I win you I I I I I I
I I I I I I I I I I I arise
to legions of
Black Daughters
Black Sons
Black Suns
that shine that that that
that chime in the chorus
with me smiling our Black smiles
stompin our Black feet
Black like me!
Black like you
Black because you can't undo me
cant poo poo me or shoo me away
I AM YOU
you made me
out of the dust and lust combusted
I am your most trusted
adversary, I know you and
you can't know me no
see My Black Daddy gave me
gone Daddy gone
Who sang that song? I am here today and
every day is my birthday when
I say Black like hell Black my
shell Black I dwell Black anger
dwells in me
Black stones Black roots Black
shoots Black seas Black trees

Black seeds.
      seeds.
I'm spewing this Black oil crude out of my hands
and out of the sands Black knuckles
pain Black hands are strained

I love you, Black Self.
I love you, Black Me.
I love you, Black Sheep.
I love you, Black She.

Jimmie Ware

Jimmie Ware is a poet and advocate for women's empowerment. She is featured in *Chicken Soup for the Soul's Curvy and Confident.* She is a former radio personality on KFAT 92.9 in Anchorage and founder of the Black Feather Poets, Inc. Ms. Ware currently resides in Phoenix, Arizona. She is published in *Southwest Persona Poems, Bearing the Mask.* She is a voice for the voiceless and gives back with passion and purpose.

OUR GLORIOUS TRUTH

Reclaim your throne

Gather the goddess garments

Adorn the trinkets and complete the cipher

Hold your head up and wipe away the tears

We have shed the required amount for cleansing

Forgive the mistake and hold fast to the lessons

Let your spirit soar

Claim your crowns and reconnect with Mother Earth

Father time shows no mercy so make haste

Teach the little sisters and heed the warnings of our fore-mothers of all colors

Embrace wisdom — life is short — live wisely

Give from your heart and uplift with your words

Let your lips speak life, love, and intelligence

Let not your hands or thoughts be idle for there is work to be done

The village needs repair and the vineyard is ripe

We are warrior women — strong and beautiful — diligent in our quest

Yes, we have much to do

Your mirror does not lie, why should you?

Your eyes observe the truth, exercise your brain

Educate your mind and accept no wooden nickels

We get what we believe we deserve, aim higher

Excuses are useless — know your worth — saying "no" is fine

If not aligned with your program, if they don't understand

Say "no ma'am or no sir"— it is not okay to be used

Some have it twisted, that means confused

To all things there is a season

Even this piece has reason

It is to honor who we are

To reconnect with our dreams

To raise self-respect and self-esteem

Queen

Realize you are regal

Adorn yourself in luxurious joy

Love yourself deeply and she will love you back and guide

Your steps towards happiness you have yet to know

We give too much/take too little and cry too often

It is time for self-time to rise — dry your eyes

Free your splendid soul, the way Queens tend to do

The Fairytale is over/a new chapter has just begun…

JIMMIE WARE

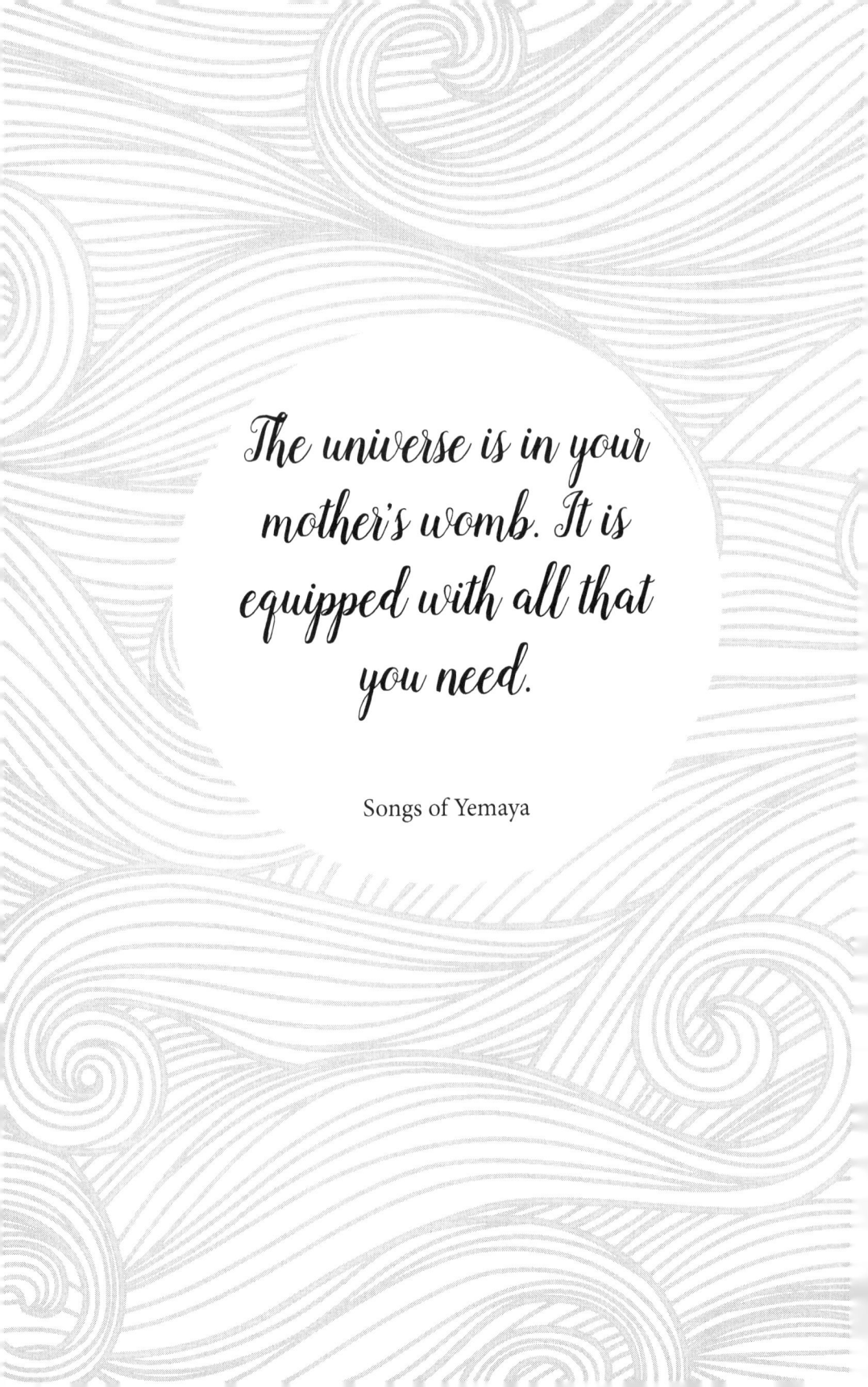

The universe is in your mother's womb. It is equipped with all that you need.

Songs of Yemaya

MAMI WATA CRADLES

When you were in the stretch of my stomach,
I dreamt. Dreamt of a time when you would run
Through bougainvillea and chirp to the song of
Crickets. Of the days you'd climb guava trees and
Curl your toes into dusty red earth as soldier ants
Convoyed past. Of your smile as butterflies basked
In the heady humid air of spectacular yellow
Coctu, Purple Hibiscus, and cooking-pot stew.
But now my stomach retches at the taste of
Bitter mendacity and the disquieting,
Dismemberment of you.

Drained like your clay-pot, Mama,
I was dry of blood.

Beheld in the River Thames as sodden bobbing tore
Bereft of bearings or bushes,
They called me Afro-Caribbean:

I could have been.
We've shared a limbo dance and more.

They later thought seven half-candles and a sheet to the waves
Tied me to the charmed blue ilk of Adekoye Adeoye
But it did not
For he, the honourable Fola, was found drumming
Rhapsodic reprieve from twin tower eclipse
Of shock and awe. My fate,

Until they found me ten days later,
Was a lonely grave by the muddy banks
Of Tower Bridge and Globe Theatre.

No mother of comfort to weep my departure -
Mama, you could not have known I was there.

No heat reflected off cracked asphalt or
Burnt amber roads to warm my watery tomb,

No fresh sticky scent of squeezed ripe mango or
The pound, pound, pound of fufu to
Entice and guide me on my way.

Not even two minutes of silence.

What kind of Elegbara was called upon
By my guardians,
Murdering cohort of three,
To spin me up
                and
                    down
Through sewage-ridden waves
The colour of fireless coal
In the deep deep sleep of night?

And *she*,
How could *she* name me Ikpomwosa?
What lies! What irony! Ogun I swear
My spirit will haunt her.

And you, Bawa Juju, I watched your face.
Trusting, I drank of the cup and ate of the bread.
With the curiosity of an innocent child peering into
The narrow neck of a large earthenware pot
I stared into the pit of your eyes without knowing
Their dark hollow expanse would soon be pouring
With the sweat of sawing exertion. I did not know
My frothing, gulping scream would not echo.
Could not echo. Could not even sound.
Poisoned and paralyzed my terror
Stood blank in the light of an impotent moon,
The tongues that bubbled incantations
And shadows that danced among the splashes of potent
Ogogoro, scented oils, sea-shells and breath-blown chalk dust,
Corn, candlesticks and fleeing bright
Bright powders.

Bawa Juju you accused me of witchcraft,
Fatal punishment for a word I did not understand.
I should feel pity for your worthless soul,
Instead I rage. You stole from me.
Forest elephant, pale-fronted Negro finch, hyena,
Bush baby, yellow-throated cuckoo, cuckoo
And red river hog.
All dreams drowned by your insatiable greed
Or were they eaten by the fishermen who
Did not care for my love of Eba and Egusi Soup
Boiled yam and Ogbono?
Or my grandmother's Owo Ovwri:
For there is no smoked fish

In the River Thames
Only leaves of bitter tricks.

But limbo is not forever.
Mami Yemoja rocks me in my watery grave,
Cradles my faithfulness, whispers my spirit-name:
"Olokun, Olokun, Olokun"
Yes, I am Olokun and I, Bawa Juju,
Will find you.

And so yes, I swear, Bawa Juju, I will find you.

L'Angela Honeysuckle Moon Lee

L'Angela Honeysuckle Moon Lee is a Louisiana handcraft artisan, apothecary, herbalist and more based in Atlanta, Georgia. She is a true daughter of nature, a rebel butterfly gazer. Since 2005, she's served local and global communities as Chief Product Developer of Honeysuckle Moon Natural Skin Care. Honeysuckle Moon with a kaleidoscopic portfolio as an apothecary and natural artist is a budding nature photographer and writer. *Love War Struggle* (2004) is her first self-published collection of poetry and meditative visualization. As an apothecary, she began creating organic spa recipes inside of her Mama's kitchen in her humble, bayou town and birthplace, Bastrop, Louisiana. Today, she continues that very important work. Mama Honeysuckle Moon knows that it is an essential duty of life to serve the Most High Jah by providing excellent service to the people, while standing in her African and Indigenous ancestors' love, cosmological intelligence, healing abilities and overall connection to nature.

SPIRIT OF WOMAN

When it thunders
In your ears
Is the message that moans for tomorrow
When the lightning
Ignites the sky
It is my labor that
Strikes and recites the song of sorrow
I am the wisdom faculty
Resting within the wife
I am the rhythm for the race of Life
I am the treasure chest
Who bears no price
I am the original sacrifice

It is I who inspires the
Trunks of trees
I am the soul rebel
Who rocks the roots and reggae
Through the tributaries of the I-3's
I am the place where
Abyssinian mystery systems hid
I've pranced the peaks of
The Great Pyramids
It is I who danced diamond cuts
Into the foundation of Menkaura
Khafra… Khufu…
I am the Original Voodoo
Vodun
Oshun
I am the motivation and personification
Of the Moon

Life is a must
As I receive the thrust of trust
One becomes nine
As wetness drips
From the mind
Irrigating the spine
My stretchmarks are a
Sign of the Divine...
My stretchmarks are a
Sign of the Divine
I am the circle
Waiting for straight lines
I pushed
Making the Sun in my likeness
I pushed
Giving birth to twin galaxies
Despite the fallacy
That's being conveyed to our
Community

Technology stays mad at me
Because despite war
I still bring forth Life
Despite hate
I still bring forth Life
Despite prophylactics and
Abortion scare tactics
I still bring forth Life
Despite death
I still bring forth Life

Self-preservation
Is the soul's motivation
For the continuance of procreation
This nation has not
Established a situation that's
Conducive to me
She's placed cuffs on my mind
She's put my words behind bars
Ill attempts to arrest and oppress my thoughts
Which confirm the
Story-telling star's account that
It is I who birthed Ausar
Infinite
Yet empty effort
All to keep me from
Freedom

Luisah Teish

Luisah Teish is a storyteller-writer, an artist-activist, and spiritual guidance counselor based in Oakland, California. She is an initiated elder (Iyanifa) in the Ifa/Orisha tradition of the West African Diaspora. She is the author of *Jambalaya: The Natural Woman's Book of Personal Charms and Practical Rituals*, and she co-authored *On Holy Ground: Commitment and Devotion to Sacred Land* with Kahuna Leilani Birely. She has contributed to 35 anthologies and has articles in *Coreopsis: Journal of Myth and Theater* and the *Cascadia Subduction Zone Journal of Speculative Fiction*. Her most recent work is *Spirit Revealing, Color Healing*, a book of Zen Doodles. She teaches online courses, facilitates conferences and weekend workshops, and performs in theaters worldwide.

YEMAYA-OLOKUN

Yemaya-Olokun is the Mother of the Sea, the Great Water, the Womb of Creation. She is the Mother of Dreams, the Mother of Secrets. She is natural wealth, the Mother of Pearl and Veiled Isis. She is the mermaid, the full moon, and intelligence beyond human comprehension.

She is envisioned as a large and beautiful woman, radiant and dark; nurturing and devouring; crystal clear and mysteriously deep.

Yemaya rules the house, nurtures the child in the waters of the womb, and has jurisdiction over the affairs of women. The sensuous belly dance of the Middle East is a tribute to Her waves. "The Constantly Coming Woman."

Gaze upon the waters of Yemaya for your own self's sake. Perform rituals on the ocean at sunrise and midnight for your healing. Watch Her shimmering in the light of the full moon and be renewed. There is no mountain of trouble that Yemaya cannot wear down; no sickness of heart that She cannot wash clean; no desert of despair that She cannot flood with hope.

Come, my sisters, embrace Her! Feel her spray on your face! Inhale her mist! Power is the name of the Yemaya-Olokun.

Nichelle Marie Calhoun

D.C. native and daughter/granddaughter of the Great Migration via the Carolinas, Georgia, and Virginia, Nichelle Marie Calhoun is a black history/black culture enthusiast. She has traveled throughout Central America, volunteering, working and collecting stories of Afro-diasporic experiences. When she is stateside, she works as a communications manager doing outreach in Miami's communities and advancing race and equity initiatives within her organization. She has freelanced as a travel writer for the online magazine, *Nubia*, published in *Walking in the Feminine: A Stepping Into Our Shoes Anthology*, and hosted her own online poetry show.

PASSING DOWN

It's the end of life now.

That is what the doctors say. I am stunned to see her so thin. She is sheer like curtains, and I see the beginning of her. I feel like I know her like no one else at that moment, but in reality, I know nothing except that life is fleeting and that the one who appears closest to death might be the one most alive. Living has imprinted that lesson on me.

She is my grandmother, Lillian Marshall Smoot McClain, Warrenton, Virginia born, the lightest of yellows, freckled with brown marks and moles, caped with hair so loosely waved and long that we seem opposites, unrelated. I am an infinity browner, and the Nigerian accented caretaker asks me if I even belong to her.

I do.

I am her Washingtonian legacy. I, Nichelle Marie Calhoun, brush out her long hair. It is black and white and in perfect balance, causing little resistance. She doesn't flinch like I do. Her hair does not snag like cheap pantyhose like mine. Grandma Lillian melts into the tenderness, and I realize just how much the aging process isolates touch—makes it sparse and elusive. It is caring for and not caring. As I brush her hair, my grandmother's eyes focus downward as she uses the last bits of herself to push and pull at my flea market-bought wallet.

I am encouraged by the interest, a sign of life.

My eight-year-old daughter Emma is in the room, too. She knows my grandmother better than I do now, and she is quick to remind me of that fact.

Emma has seen Lillian much more than I have and lets me know with adult-like clarity that she actually goes to church with my mother on a Sunday, routinely followed up with a visit to the nursing home after. Emma speaks with an honesty that only belongs to someone still so close in age to God. It fully implies that I would not be so shocked by my grandmother's condition had I showed up at church a little more often.

I do not wince at not attending church.

I wince at the breach between generations, between two women linked by blood but whose existence depended so unevenly on each other. I, indebted to living, and she, graced only by these final acts of compassion, near death. We never knew each other really; we were only the lightest breezes on each other's lives outside of these facts.

I cannot write her story. I cannot explain her inner reasons to not raise her children six times over. I cannot save my own mother the hidden grief of explaining why her mother did not offer her the culture and geography of a mother's love. I cannot write a damn thing about Lillian Marshall Smoot McClain of Warrenton, Virginia, except that I am here.

I can, however, write about staying up on Friday nights looking for leads on genealogical websites; searching through census documents, birth and death certificates; piecing together stories of people in records who have gone on; visiting the archives at the Afro-American Historical Association of Fauquier County; and taking a DNA test introducing me to new relatives and confirming all the historical humiliations a black women could fear during enslavement.

I can talk about the sense of justice in searching and discovering, how every re-creation of a skeleton narrative based on birth and death date, location, name, race, rent or own, literate or illiterate placed my mother and myself in time, in history, in unknown family legacies, and within a historical narrative.

I can talk about a 1920s photo of my great-grandparents: sepia, worn, collected from the belongings of my now nursing home-bound grandmother some years prior. I can mention how I had seen that picture in passing many times before when my mother would take me to visit my grandmother pre-nursing home days at her Connecticut Avenue apartment. I can elaborate on how I would look at the faces but never connected that I belonged to them: two lovers turned spouses. My great-grandfather dark, poreless, smooth in a suit, seated, legs crossed, hand lightly resting on the family dog in the picture; and my great-grandmother standing, plain, beige-skinned, spectacled, dressed in a house dress and pearls.

I can share how I reached out to the Fauquier County Historical Society in Warrenton, Virginia, two years prior, wanting them to center the worn sepia picture on the white-washed website charged with telling the story of the county. I can report back that there was no evidence of "color" on that site—no sepia, no mahogany, no gamut of sun-baked yellows, no black Smoot, Bailey, Lawson, Marshall, Craig. The picture I held—proof of life, proof of a lie.

I can expound on how the outreach to the Fauquier County Historical Society put me on a path to the Afro-American Historical Association of Fauquier County, a red-bricked house with photos, records, and artifacts collected by a determined local black anthropologist committed to putting blackness back into the region's narrative. I can gratefully commit to explain that with the society's help, I reached back to 1771 to Betsey, a rumored enslaved American Indian woman and spy during the Revolutionary War. I can put forth that the papers that I held at the society say that Betsey had a son, John Lawson, and that John Lawson would marry Mary Richardson, both with black blood and free, born 1817 and 1820, respectively. I can admit that I breathed a sigh of relief that they were accounted for on the 1830 census because most African-Americans were not accounted for on any census records until 1870. It was only when slavery was abolished that they would be considered human enough to be counted.

Proof of freedom.

The written historical account in the Afro-American Historical Association can attest John Lawson and Mary Richardson had Francis Lawson, and that Francis Lawson would marry Jake Woodward, born 1848 and 1851, respectively. Both free. Frances and Jake would have Mary Lawson in 1877. Mary Lawson would marry Henry Bailey. As a result of that union, Mary Lawson and Henry Bailey had Rachel Bailey, born in 1896. Rachel Bailey is the beige-skinned woman standing next to her husband, my great-grandfather, in that sepia photo before the birth of my grandmother Lillian, who is now dying as I brush her salt and pepper hair.

246 years later, my earliest known root and I intersect here with the oldest living member of that line, my grandmother. We are here together, finally. I know her now as I brush her hair. I know that Lillian wanted tenderness, wanted a place in the now, wanted a place in history. The beginning of this known maternal line, an enslaved woman named Betsey, down to its youngest member—my daughter—and the woman who is the likeliest bridge between this world and the next, my grandmother.

I know her too little. I know her too late. I know her in time.

I say her name with all of the black women whose stories have been lost. A mother of six, Lillian becomes synonymous with the choice of not following through on motherhood in family narratives. I have the luxury of not blaming her. I have the luxury of searching. I have the luxury of preserving what she has passed down. Life.

We meet here.

I say thank you and write her name into forever.

A TALE BASED ON OLOKUN'S INSPIRATION

Once there was a beautiful woman by the name of Ye-ma-ya, who looked into the waters of the ocean. There she saw Her own reflection and asked, "Who is that beautiful woman? I thought that I was the prettiest thing that the World had ever seen!"

And as She looked on that woman there came a rumbling in Her belly and it grew, and it grew, and it grew until it exploded and covered the lands with lakes, rivers, and streams. Yemaya looked into the water of the river and there, again, she saw that woman and asked, "Who is that beautiful woman? I thought that I was the prettiest thing that the World had ever seen!"

And again, Her belly grew, and it grew and grew till it exploded and sprinkled the heavens with stars and a full moon. Yemaya looked in the full moon, and again she asked, "Who is that beautiful woman? I thought that I was the prettiest thing that the World had ever seen!" And again, Her belly grew, and it grew, and it grew until it exploded! And before Her stood thousands of beautiful women.

Yemaya asked, "Who are you, beautiful women? I thought that I was the prettiest thing that the World had ever seen!" The women looked deep into the Eyes of Yemaya, and there they saw their own reflections.

So the women said to Yemaya, "You are! We're just you!"

NLisah

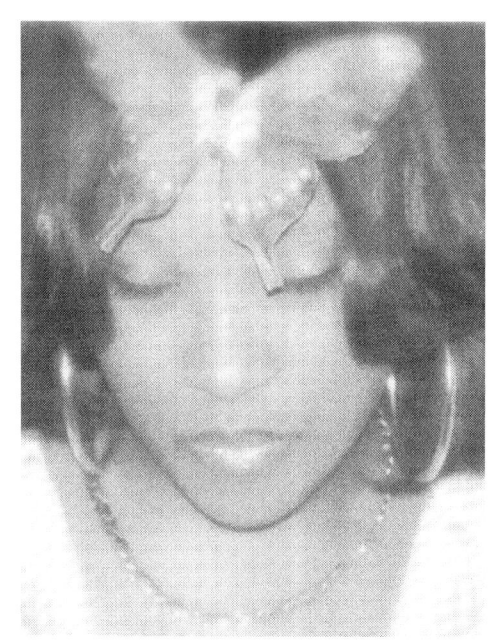

Nifeesia Harris also known as published author NLisah is a mother of five based in Philadelphia, Pennsylvania. She is the owner of Black Buttafly Publishing Company. NLisah is actively writing her second book, *Life, Trials and Love*. Before finding her wings in writing, she explored many career paths working as a correctional officer, deputy sheriff officer and an outreach worker serving the homeless. Today, along with writing and striving in entrepreneurship, she continues to work in human services coordinating, helping and assisting the homeless population of Philadelphia.

WE LEARNED, THEY TAUGHT, I TEACH

They taught me well,
this I do know
One taught character
and another taught me why I must not fail.

I became an observer with her help
I became unique, indestructible like concrete
I saw by her trips and falls to gravitate towards standing tall
I saw by her dependency to remember Me.
I saw hurt and pain
as she listened to Oldies and had private conflicts with cocaine.
I saw her heart as she helped everyone whom she could reach
I saw her pass away with unfulfilled dreams, too
I saw her struggles as she tried her hardest
I saw her be the only woman in a house full of brothers.
I saw her try to fit in
as she and her mother butted heads often.
Ambushed by hurt and pain made it seem best to sit
I saw a strong woman who just didn't know where she fit.
And I saw the older matriarch, too
Retired and now had to raise one more
Introduction to books, theater and finer things was now in store.
The matriarch gained a chance at redemption it seems
She could assist her only daughter's child while fulfilling prophecy.
She held many regrets from her past
If only she had devoted time and Love to the child's mother when she had
But at least she was given another pass
To introduce this child to all brand new
To not show contempt or judgement
To redeem her past mistakes

She would nurture the child to introduce newness and great.
Make the next generation after something better.

So, she taught class and style
She taught tailored shoes with heel tips
She taught if nothing kind then refrain your lips.
She taught profanity never should come out of a lady
She taught dress up for holidays and often on other occasions
She taught always save money and have your own
She taught never cry ever unless you're alone.
She taught Christmas as a time for decoration and flair
As you breeze through downstairs and smell pine cones in the air.
She taught reading as a fundamental principle
She taught vacation often because your life and enjoyment is valuable.
She taught sophisticated ways
She taught entrepreneurship
She taught valuable is actually a look.

She never taught how to fix inside when life shook the theories that be.

But now I teach!
As I have three little ladies of my own,
Teaching them life lessons to attribute to the phrase "I'm Grown!"
And I introduce all of the teachings but add a few spins of my own.
I teach how to repair and strengthen inside
I teach that integrity and self-esteem
doesn't fall from a tree
I teach that you apply effort to improve where you feel weak
I teach that you separate yourself
from all unnecessary nonsense.
I teach that you value yourself
I teach to chart new roads even if you chart them alone

I teach to forget about clothes and the jazzy flair of things and to
Make your insides solid even when you see no use
because it will be needed later to propel you.

I teach strong wills, independent stands and correct and safe boundaries
I teach that you are whole already and that
Peace, life and happiness doesn't come from a man
I teach to reach for your dreams even if you fall
At least you fall to display your efforts to all.

I teach always value and see the beauty in you
Whether dark-skinned, light-skinned, brown or yellow
We are all beautiful in different hues and your uniqueness equals value.

I teach no need for jealousy
That corrupt fruit is when you think similar can't happen for you
I teach to sing, dance or race around like a fool
Just keep being you despite whoever's view.
I teach strange and odd is something to be admired
I teach strange and odd is something the "not so real kids" say
I teach you are made for success
You are a shine all your own
A beauty and a gift is
you
Never let the world steal your uniqueness and confidence implanted in you
We learned, they taught and now I teach!

And this dedication is made to my three little ladies!

SINGLE MOM-NESS

The hardest job ever.

Learning as I go, This Queen is clever.

Not perfect and I'm done crying.

I will be by your side or die trying.

Sensuality is loving the details of living.

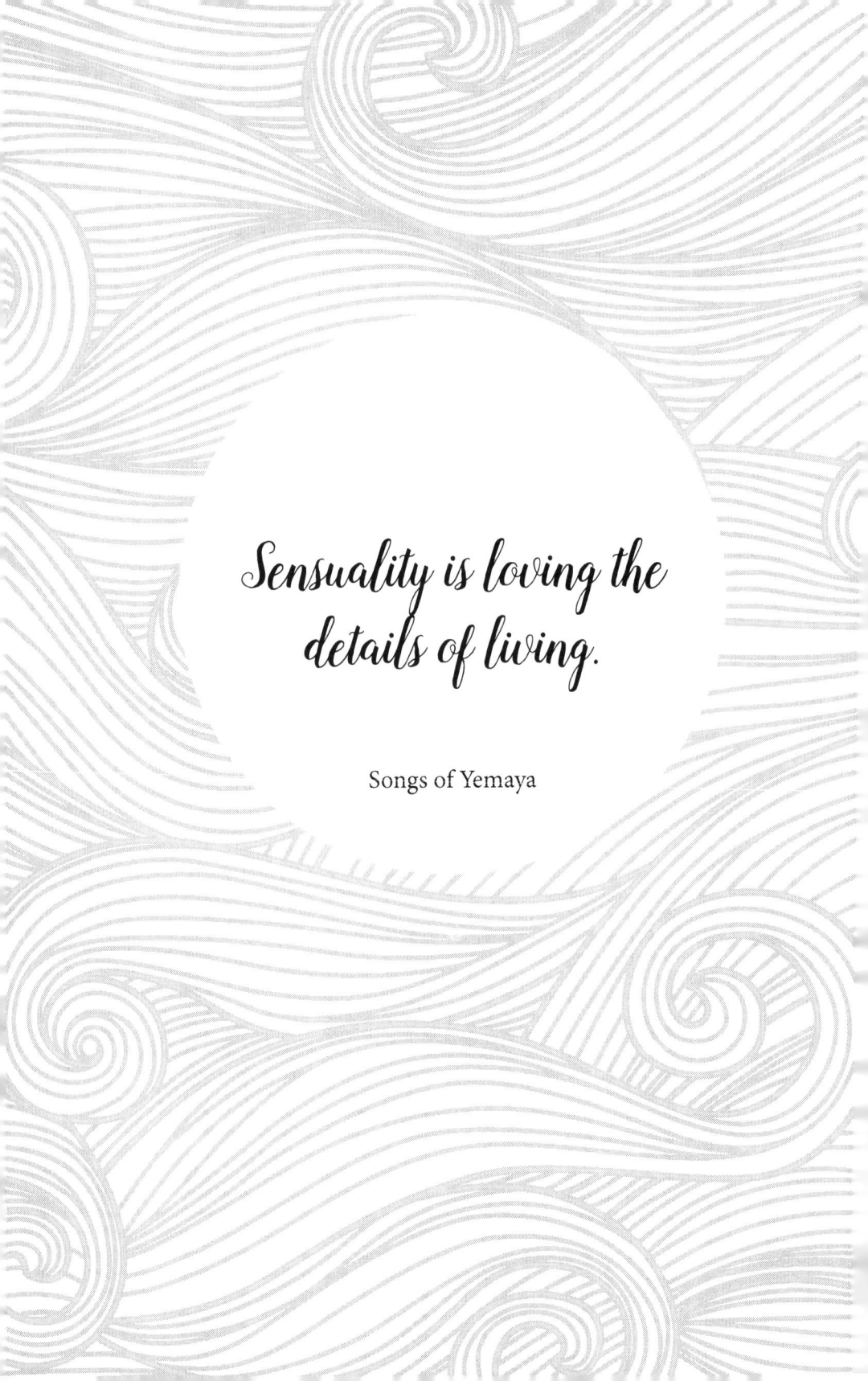

Songs of Yemaya

KIN TO NIGHT MUSIC

I am kin to night music

A deep, down darkness

An ebony baritone

Dripping from piano keys.

Oh how it sings a memory

A rumbling over dusky doorways

Arched, yawning a sleepy greeting

A welcome to coco mango women

That smell too sweet for heaven

And burn too hot for hell,

So they be sultry earth creatures.

I crave twirling wrists on fingertips,

A palm appraising pose

An exposed lower back

Leaning in and letting go

Crave hands that know their place

And heels that never touch the ground

Lusungu Kayani-Stearns

Lusungu Kayani-Stearns was born in Dar es Salaam, Tanzania, and grew up in the suburbs of Washington, D.C. After finishing college in Maryland, Lusungu lived, worked, and traveled across Africa, Asia, and parts of Latin America. She is an urban planner and passionate about cities and sustainability. She is a devoted yogini, who loves to hike and explore Mama Earth. Lusungu is constantly seeking ways to care for our world's most vulnerable humans. Lusungu received her B.A. from the University of Maryland, College Park, and a M.A. in International Affairs from the School of International and Public Affairs at Columbia University. She currently resides in New Jersey with her husband and their two wonderful and inquisitive sons.

MORNING SONG

I heard you.

It was the first time.

Loud and very clear

Would you believe it was against my vein

That I felt your beat?

My arm, high in a morning stretch

Closing my eyes for that last-minute dose of surprise

Splendidly did I count

As fast as I could

Tried to make a guess but couldn't keep up

As your heart beat in sync with mine

My luck to be a woman

And the joy to carry you

Many beats we will share together

A bum bum a bum bum a bum bum

Celeta Hickman

Celeta Hickman is a retired performer, having been a principal dancer for Nego Gato Capoeria de Angola of Bahia Brazil, Shades of Black Movement and the Legacy Arts Project—both of Pittsburgh. Ms. Hickman has presented scholarly work focusing on Africana arts, creative movement, and early childhood development domestically and internationally. Celeta's visual art has been featured in exhibits by Women of Vision, the Society of Yoruba Bead Artists, and the Three Rivers Arts Festival. She is celebrating her sixth year as the Afro-Caribbean dancer in residence at the Hill Dance Academy Theatre in Pittsburgh. She is the founder of the Ujamaa Collective a cooperative wealth building incubator artisan boutique (Ujamaa Boutique).

YOUNG YEMAYA 7 OCEANS OF BLUE

Young birds are aflutter with waves of light.

Newly washed water movement

Tranquil and tempestuous

Raging and Rocking

Mother of liquid vastness

Gushing rolling announcing

New life

Olodo

A generous welcoming nurse

Young birds learning to fly

In blue above and blue below

Foam sand and blue green weeds potent

In their medicine

Newly washed water spray

refreshing young mothers

rejuvenating old ones

baptizing the masses

Young birds with fluid spirit wings.

Mystical blue depths,

powerful mothers,

your comforting embrace,

heralding new beginnings,

a knowing nurturer,

your energy, your power,

desired, required and sought,

the world over.

Maferefun Yemaya.

THE MAKING OF A WOMAN

Give her love
Give her enough of
  You —
to make her feel secure

And every seed
of sympathy
Will bleed
  Into pleasure

No importance
The size of the matter
No need to be her slave
Or her master

Love only
Will swerve
Crippled Venus
Into stature and flesh

You withhold
the power to please
within
  The caress of your hand

Tania Saintil (Deliverance-NOIRE)

Daughter to her resilient Haitian immigrant mother, Marie Bernadette, and mother to her brilliant daughter, Dominique Zora, Tania Saintil (Deliverance-NOIRE) uses her Haitian Caribbean descendency to inspire her words and call-to-action via poetry. With a B.A. in Literary Voices from CUNY, she writes with her ancestors in central view, challenging and embracing cultural norms. She is a licensed nurse during the day, but a full-time writer returning to her craft via *Songs of Yemaya*.

SPOKEN HANDS

Two hands interconnect

like a plait of hair, double strand twist. It binds.

A woman lies on her back; she has been there before.

Hands interlace, as if in prayer. Has heaven been found?

A woman lies on her back; she has been there before.

A moment of passion shared, a symbol of union

Hands interlock, silence, no need for words.

Hands communicate, intercourse; these hands speak without moving.

The answer is in the middle of it.

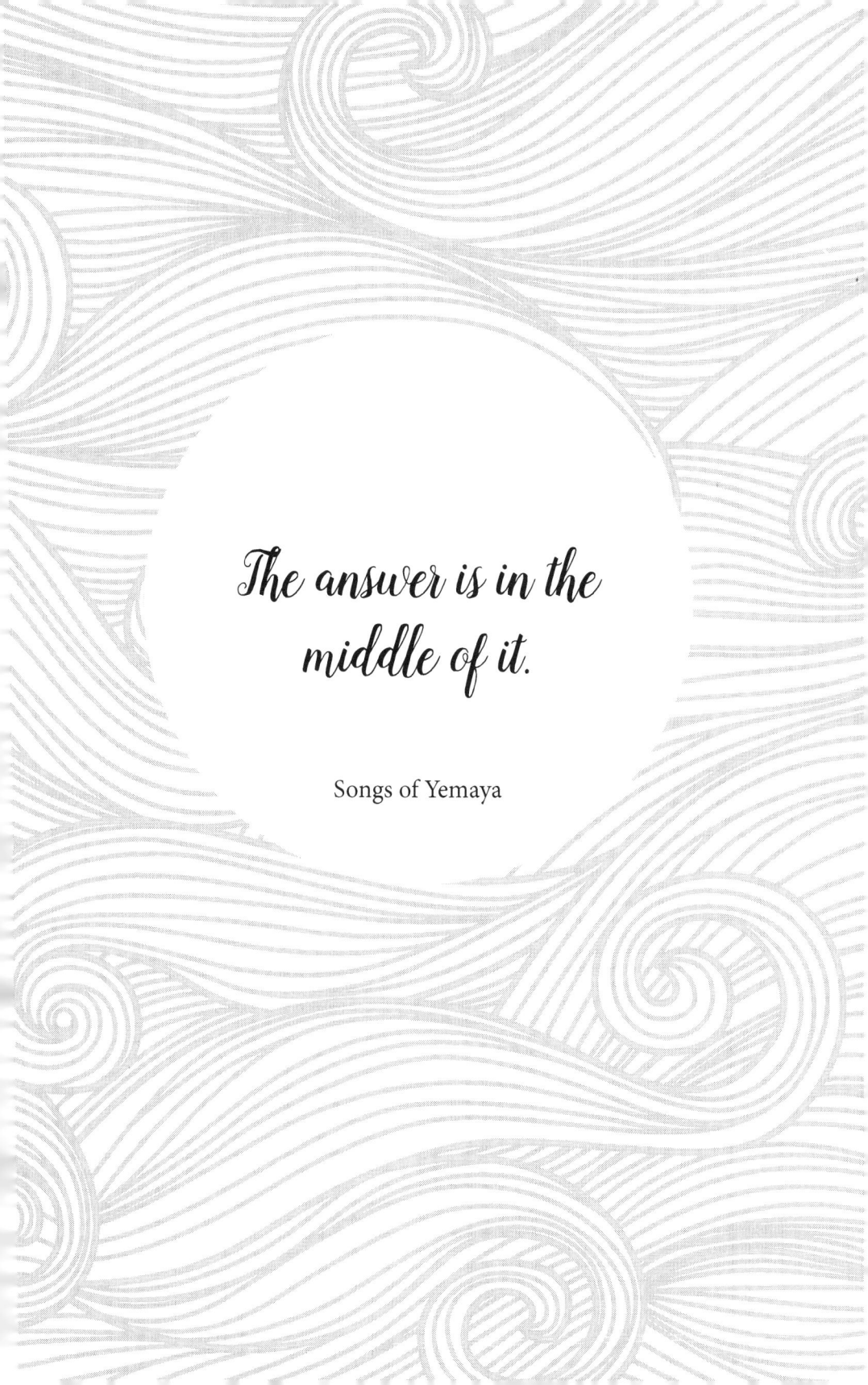

Songs of Yemaya

Althea Romeo-Mark

Born in Antigua, West Indies, Althea Romeo-Mark is an educator and writer who grew up in St. Thomas, US Virgin Islands. She has lived and taught in St. Thomas, Virgin Islands, USA; Liberia (1976-1990); London, England (1990-1991); and in Switzerland, since 1991. She was awarded the *Marguerite Cobb McKay Prize* by the Editorial Board of *The Caribbean Writer* in June 2009 for her published short story *Bitterleaf* in Volume 22, 2008. Her last poetry collection, *If Only the Dust Would Settle,* was published in 2009. Her poem, *Lost Love*, was originally published in the anthology *Women in War: (Protest Against Gender Violence)* by CWC, Gambia, in 2015.

LOST LOVE

(for Liberia on its Independence Day, July 26)

I have left you, was forced to leave you,
'cause you pushed me away.

Had I remained, I might be speaking
from a shallow, leaf-draped grave
somewhere in a forest in the company of the dead
who did not wish to flee, could not flee your side.

There are those who survived the bi-polar rage
that boiled in your blood and corrupted bones.
They subsisted on cunning, prayers and small miracles.

This conflict was not of your making.
The clashing voices within
tore you asunder. And you fell apart,
unable to pacify warring schisms—
old souls rejecting a tainted new,
new souls subjugating the old.

Scarred by your fury,
many do not wish to replant their loyalty
only to be felled like unwanted timber.
Many who live in your shadow
still reel from the fear that became their life.

Some spin senseless tales on how
to make you better, on how to cure your ills.
And there are homegrown carpetbaggers
playing chess with your future,
ready to flee at the first signs of fire-storm.

Perhaps I will visit, skirt around your tantrums,
but I have been burned and will not stay.
I chose life over deadly love. I am in the arms
of another who brings calm to my spirit.
I will not throw this away.

SUMMER STORY

The kind of summer when your favorite jeans rip
Too easily in the pockets
You notice yourself coming apart at the seams
Learn that you can fool yourself
forgive yourself
forbid yourself from ever doing this again.

When you realize - truly realize -
that you control nothing but yourself,
no one but yourself,
know no one but yourself.
Realize you are not now alone
you have always been alone -
alone with your thoughts, feelings, fears,
indecencies, ellipses.
And that alone is not some cold, dark place.
It is permanent. It is home. It is always.

When you cloister away in your apartment
forsaking what lies without for the promise of what lies within.
the goal being not selling yourself short,
not using your body to silence your mind,
not putting your heart out in the middle of the street to get run over.
The goal being to respect yourself,
to treat yourself better, kinder, gentler, with greater deference.
It's an act of self-preservation, an act of resistance,
resisting patterns so old and tattered they're good for nothing other
than to be thrown away.

This summer sounds like power ballads.

This summer smells like burning.

This summer looks like clouds rolling in.

This summer tastes like salt.

This summer feels like solid ground beneath your feet.

The story of this summer is one of coming home.

To friends and food and family

Of seeing with eyes old and new what's true, what's you.

When you draw the focus inward and burst forth from the solar plexus,

from the sacrum,

from the soul,

with pure unfiltered freedom.

Throwing off the shackles of your sadness,

self-doubt, and supplicancy

to scream,

and run, and be,

believing,

truly, that the best has only just begun.

Rashida James-Saadiya

Rashida James-Saadiya is a visual artist, writer, and cultural educator invested in transforming spaces and social perceptions through collective art-making. Her work addresses otherness, aesthetics and the complexities of Brown womanhood in America. In addition, she is the Creative Director of Crossing Limits, an interfaith non-profit organization utilizing poetry as an instrument of beautification and agent for social change, highlighting the intersections of faith and social injustice.

SELF-PRESERVATION LOVE NOTES

The moment you awake it begins: meals to prepare, children to dress, emails to return, and a to-do list that never ends. There are possibly countless words to define this state of frenzy, yet the word "busy" seems to fit perfectly. In a recent conversation with a close friend who is also a mother to small children, we spent at least an hour comparing our daily, overwhelming schedules. In these moments, "busy" feels like some strange form of adult success—or at least some stand-in for productivity. I felt exhausted after our talk, and was forced to remind myself that being "busy" was never a life goal. I realized that "busy" is simply a state of mind—a state that often causes stress, low energy, and unhappiness. I needed to redefine my definition of success and this hectic path I willingly accepted as normal. There will be no shiny gold award for most overwhelmed and overworked. At the end of our lives, we will all be the same amount of awesome dust. I asked myself: How much joy was I bringing into my life and what efforts, if any, was I taking to actually enjoy the sheer blessing of being alive? Confident that life should be filled with more than exhaustion, I began the journey of reminding myself that I am here to build relationships, experience life, go places, create things, and laugh often.

Admittedly, it's difficult to exist in a state of "busy" while balancing family and learning to consistently nurture my well-being. This complexity has shown me the importance of taking time to outline and revisit values and ways of being that are essential to my personal growth. Is it having calm mornings? Is it learning the art of saying "no?" Or is it practicing better forms of self-care? Just because I can, doesn't mean I should; the key cause of "busy" is simply trying to accomplish too much. It's easy to pack my weekends with errands, household cleaning, science projects, and social activities. When did I forget that weekends were sacred? While productivity is certainly important, my body has rights over me; this means that I must not labor without taking time to rejuvenate and restore my spirit. While spending the entire weekend in a hammock with my favorite book is unrealistic, there is profound beauty in remembering that rest and relaxation are essential to problem solving, well-being, and spiritual balance.

Doing less is easier said than done. It requires a radical shift. The idea that the quality of my life, well-being, happiness, sense of joy, and fulfillment are enhanced when I do less, not more, is a radical departure from social norms. Yet, I am all too familiar with the painful complications of forgetting to honor my needs. The practice of slowing down, especially when my plate is full, is like using a secret weapon, or sending myself a beautiful love note. Take deep breaths and remember, sometimes slower is better. Be gentle with yourself.

A SURVIVOR'S DILEMMA

Misconceptions
Based on race, ethnicity, complexion
And my self-proclaimed Womanist identity
Coupled with the microaggressions
Such as requests to see my transcripts and course lists
Apparently a degree will not suffice
When my ability and educational competency
Remains in question
And I receive questions
About how I came to be so ambitious
Considering my heritage
My family's place of origin
Leads to ignorant questions
And assumptions
That regularly roll off the tongues of assholes
Compounding my daily struggles

Which I often fight in silence
For verbalizing your most inner thoughts can be dangerous
Because accumulated microaggressions
Can give rise to thoughts of violence

Then there is that issue of street harassment
The verbal and the far too often physical violence
I cannot take a few steps down a city street
Without someone coming forth with disrespect
Without being objectified
And within my community there is the familiar call of
Psst Psst
Sweet things
With calls to let strange men
Strangers
Just touch Dat Ting
The rounded caboose
That I cannot even hide in business suits
Dat Ting

THELONIUS MONK PLAYS AGAIN

A smothered moan, ruffling of crisp newly washed sheets.

"Are you ok (pause, swallow (gulp)), Mommy?"

A sob is caught in my throat

A lump forms, can't swallow.

My senses are up, sweat pours, and armpits itch

Single drop of sweat hits my chest, PLOOP!

Pulse erratic, Thelonius Monk is playing in my chest walls again.

Uncontrollable, all over the place, no one rhythm, all-alternating.

It is happening again. Thought he would have stayed out longer,

The routine, come in stumbling, drop on bed, THUD, pass out.

Not tonight, I'm scared.

I smell it, familiar (sour, nasty spoiled, acidic, bile rising, bitter, raunchy) smell of Vodka.

I can sniff it out, better than a Russian working on a potato farm.

It holds so many memories.

Full of broken promises.

Endless nights of talking to God

Inhibitions formed,

Hesitant reaction to affection,

Sought power of the written word.

Words that can evoke emotions,

Pain, lust, eroticism, religion:

Faith found, at last.

This is how I choose to remember my father.

Maybe you are already full.

Songs of Yemaya

Nefertiti Asanti

Nefertiti Asanti is a writer, cultural worker, and sometimes performance poet from the Bronx. Her work explores healing, Afrofuturism, queerness, and womanist musings. For over a decade, she has performed original spoken word and theater pieces staged throughout NYC and beyond. Nefertiti resides in Oakland and is working on her first poetry chapbook.

THE FAMILIAR WAYS OF BROKEN PEOPLE

The broken people feel familiar
Small enough to fit in your palm
& love you for putting them there

In your hands
the broken people are useful

You think to yourself
& you say to yourself
Conditioned words
Words conditioned to soothing

Tongue stroking where it hurts
Lips sucking out the poison

Until it gets stuck inside of you
Until you're filled with a familiar broken
Until you're small enough to fit inside
someone else's palm

Only their palms are not free
& their hands are empty
Pointed fingers do not love you
The broken people are useless

So you think to yourself
and you say to yourself
Conditioned words
Words conditioned to soothing

Tongue stroking where it hurts
Lips spitting out the poison
Until you unlearn the familiar ways
of broken people.

Sileta Blu Hodge

Born in Anguilla, Sileta Blu Hodge developed an affinity for creative writing at an early age. She has published several short stories, *Harbor Town, The Black Widow,* and *Blue Jays Over Hot Porridge.* Hodge also recently released a non-fiction book on business and entrepreneurship, called *Think Outside Your Cubicle.* While indulging in her creative writing, she is usually a recluse. When it is time for play, Hodge enjoys spending time with family and traveling, and pursuing one of her favorite pastimes, sketching and painting. Presently, she is focused on completing her debut novel, *From Sugar City.*

To Sandrine and Verna

NANA'S DAUGHTERS

On the chilling night that Emily Huffington passed, I sat still for hours, peering at the movement of the shadows of the water waves against the wall. I sat there empty. Not a thought. Not an emotion. Just blank. Lady China, without permission, yawned, stretched, then walked over to me, pouring herself into my lap. We sat there together, both of us helpless, watching someone die who never lived. In fact, the only life she ever lived was through a series of romance novels she'd written under the pseudonym, Erica Forbes. Twelve of which were bestsellers.

A devout recluse, not too many would know this about her: Emily Huffington, my mother, was ineluctably arrested by the shortcomings of her past. In her last moments, I held her cold fingers between the spaces of mine. Barely responsive, with eyes sunken between deep sockets, she held back with the little life she had left. Meanwhile, the lake's current picked up its pace across the wall—a wild dance, in a memorizing pattern, almost in celebration of her life.

The call came at a bad time.

I was moments away from walking on stage to speak to the upcoming senior graduating class of George Washington High, where over four-hundred students were seated in the auditorium. The principal needed someone to deliver an electrifying motivational speech to the senior class, and apparently, I was the woman for the job.

Natalia's voice was firm on the other end of the receiver, "You should come see her now. There's not much time left."

My body went ice cold and my knees wobbled, throwing me off balance backstage. When two staff members ran over and asked if I was okay, I assured them I was. One of them, a teacher named Mr. Brooks, insisted that I drink some water. The dwarf-heighted man then disappeared behind a door backstage and came back with a glass with ice and a bottle of water in the other hand. I poured some out, took a few sips, smiled to let him know I was okay, then moved slowly on to the stage.

I repeated my speech just as I had prepared for it days before. Pausing after an important message, emphasizing on critical points, and using hand gestures to keep the energy alive in the room. The adolescents interacted with me, clapping, chanting, and raving. My body was present; my mind was years behind. It took me back to a memory of me holding clothes in a bucket and passing them one by one to Emily Huffington so she could pin them to the clothing line. She was a university student at that time, pursuing a degree in creative writing. Something Nana was not too happy about. She could've been a lawyer or a doctor. But she was determined to be a writer.

In closing my speech, I lost my lines, and all I could remember at that time was Emily Huffington kneeling down before me and taking the dirty sheet out of my hands. I had dropped it in the dirt and was so sure she would beat me, I started crying. But then she said, "When you mess up, pick your mess up, wash it off, and keep moving. You're human!" It was with these words that I closed out my speech.

Swerving in and out of traffic under a shower of heavy rain, I wasn't sure I would make it to her on time. Five summers had come and gone since I had last seen her. At one traffic light, when the rain did ease a little, I noticed a woman looking at me—her face void of any expression. It was one of those stares where the mind was absent from the body. I tried to follow her eyes for as long as the light was red. Once it turned green, we both squinted at each other, suspicious that we'd read each other's minds. Then almost in one accord, we quietly tapped the gas and continued our journeys into the stormy evening.

After thinking through maybe a thousand things I could say to her, I finally pulled into my mother's driveway and parked under the shadow cast by a huge maple tree.

Not sure if anyone would be there to let me in, I thought about testing my old key in the front door. I was surprised to hear the familiar squeak as the door slowly opened, especially since I was warned by Emily Huffington herself, not to return to the property. I never thought I would return either.

At least not this soon.

Upon entering the parlor, I immediately recognized an old photo of a ten-year-old me, hanging on the wall. Next to it was a photo of Nana and me in her kitchen. If I remembered well, we were baking bread that day and mother was the one who snapped the photo.

Walking through it, I realized how much I missed this place. The ceilings were high with bamboo plastering, and the rooms were spacious. As big as the place was, the wooden touch and earth-toned colors gave off a cottage-like comfort.

I took light steps in clicking heels through the hall and made my way up the staircase where the carpet quieted the sound of my steps. On my way up, a soft ball of fur brushed between my legs, almost throwing me off balance. It was Lady China.

"China, what are you doing?!" I gritted my teeth at her.

Tail in the air, the cat ignored me and hurried to the room. She stopped before entering and slapped her tail hard against the door, letting me know that time was of the essence.

Once at the top of the stairs, a cinnamon fragrance played in my nostrils all the way to the dimly lit chamber where Emily Huffington was lying down.

Guilt-ridden, I entered the room in slow strides. Green-eyed Lady China took a seat at the edge of the bed, head down and resting on her paws. Her black coat was shiny, indicating that she was recently groomed. I was not too fond of cats, but in my absence, the stray animal grew to be mother's best friend.

To my surprise, she was awake, propped on a pillow, with a pen and worn out journal in hand. I felt her warm spirit when I entered the room, though a heaviness pulled on my heart. I couldn't believe I had managed to stay away from her for that long.

Without turning to look at me, she managed to smile, acknowledging my presence. I was shocked by how much she'd aged while she was yet so young. Her caramel cheeks, which were once plump, had disappeared, leaving only the hard frame of her cheekbones. A woman I thought I would never see in a weak and vulnerable state was dying. Her grim condition had taken away her beauty, but her soul was left unscathed. She was peaceful and content with what life had given her, yet had so much left to gain.

I removed my coat and sat next to her. After an hour of utter silence, she spoke with a strained voice I couldn't recognize.

"I knew you would come." She swallowed hard and then muttered, "Nothing worse than dying alone."

I tried not to talk or think. Everything I set my eyes on became a blur. I closed my eyes and allowed the tears to roll out as I ran my fingers through her thin hair. Hair that used to feel like thick wool between my fingers on Sunday mornings. I would clear it out for her before Nana got to it. Nana was a patient woman, but she was rough when it came to combing hair like mother's.

When I opened my eyes, I fixed my attention on the blurry cat, who by now had edged a few inches closer to its owner. I kept quiet. Mother didn't mind my silence either. Instead, she continued writing in her journal. It was in admiration that I looked on as she wrote her last thoughts. Then when she could no longer bear to move, she stared off to one side of the room, where silver draped curtains fell to a well-polished wooden floor and were drawn back to let the moonlight in.

When she did manage to speak again, she asked in a very low tone, "My granddaughter?"

The cat's ears became erect, and I knew it had heard my heartbeat speed up the moment that question was asked. How could mother have known?

I cleared my throat, "She…Her…her…name is Serenity. Just like your middle name."

It was the last time I would see her smile and cry.

The night was sad and beautiful. The faint moonlight glistened on the quiet lake out back. As the distant storm threatened the night, ripples from the rain drizzle made the lake all the more enchanting. Tears welled up in my eyes as I rested her head in my lap like she did mine when I was a little girl. I played with her hair while I hummed one of the spirituals Nana used to sing to us.

"Amazing grace, how sweet the sound…"

I was pleased to see her move her head slightly to the sound of my voice. The song was long but the moment was passing quickly. Emily Huffington was strong though. She survived the eleventh hour, and when the twelfth hour came, I could still feel her breathing. It wasn't long after though, that I watched her succumb to her greatest enemy. At that moment, I camouflaged my guilt and pain with nonchalance.

Just then, a chilling wind blew through the window and reminded me of the night we left Nana's house. I was maybe ten, and Mother shouted at me to snap on my seatbelt and stop the bawling. The back window was jammed stuck and was halfway open. The bitter cold hung on my skin as she sped through the dirt road, riding every bump. I caught a glance of her reflection in the rearview mirror. What I saw was a scared child, teary-eyed and lost. Right before she transitioned, it was this same look that covered her face.

The morning came quickly, and it found Lady China and me sleeping under the pattering of rain. It was the sound of clashing lightening that made me jump up in fright. The west wind had been blowing the rain directly through the window, soaking the wooden floor. Lifeless, Mother was still lying in my lap. Emily Huffington was dead, and there was no one to tell, except Natalia.

I placed towels in front of the window to absorb the water and proceeded to make arrangements for the funeral. Natalia was touched by the news and broke down in tears over the phone. For me, time had frozen, and the memories I had of my mother continued playing from random times in my childhood and then into my adulthood, up until the day we had our falling out.

The funeral was just as lonely as my mother had lived her life.

Natalia arrived in full black and dark shades. I wore a black dress that fell to my ankles and a wide-brimmed Victorian hat that covered my coarse hair and shaded my face. A strange man sat in the back row of the chapel with over a dozen roses that he placed on her coffin at the end of the ceremony. I never knew Mother to have a love interest or any friends at that. I assumed he was a neighbor, though by the way he was attired, in long navy blue designer coat, he looked to be a northerner or even a foreigner from France or Germany. I expected him to stop and express condolences, but he walked out of the chapel and went his way.

After the funeral, Natalia came by the house and sat in a private meeting with an attorney by the name of William who went over the endowments Emily Huffington had willed to her. Lady China was among the possessions she would leave with that day.

Almost a year passed before I revisited the lonely home I had inherited. This time I took Serenity with me. She was the secret I kept from Emily Huffington. Once she suspected I was impregnated by a man named Chad, mother grew bitter and was grieved to the point she felt she had lost her only child. In her opinion, he was not good enough for me. She complained about the dragon tattoo on his arm, the way he spoke in slang, and even criticized the way he walked. He was not welcomed around her, nor was my unplanned pregnancy. It turned out she was right though. Chad was an abusive drunk. Just as he lived his life, he died—tragically, in an accident.

I pulled up to the mini-mansion, admiring the beautiful architectural work as the over-sized gates separated. Emily Huffington had placed her vision in every part of her dream home. From the sky view in her bedroom that allowed her to watch the night sky or the falling rain, to the oleander garden, graveled walkways, and the greenest grass in the entire county. Once I helped Serenity out of her car seat, she hopped out and looked around the place in awe with me.

"Mommy, this is pretty! We should live here!"

"It is, baby. It really is. But I don't know if we can live here."

Serenity looked disappointed, but that didn't last long.

"Swings, Mommy! Look at the playground!"

I looked in the direction Serenity was pointing. This was the first time I'd noticed the shiny playground. Mother had been expecting me to return, but how could I have known?

"Mommy, can we go play? Please!" I smiled and nodded at the little ball of energy as she looked up at me while tugging at my shirt.

"We will play later on. Not now," I promised her.

I pulled dozens of letters from the mailbox and was surprised to see how many wildflowers had grown through the cracks in her driveway. I entered the home and found that it was still neatly kept, only that a little dust had settled here and there.

I lifted Serenity in my arms and spun her around into the master bedroom. She giggled the entire way, her long twists bouncing around her face.

Once in the bedroom, I noticed that the curtains were still drawn just as they were the night she passed. A father and son were standing at the edge of the lake with a fishing rod. He was leaning over the lad, who was no more than six years old. I looked on as he rested his hands over his son's, guiding him for a catch.

"Mommy I want to—fish—too!" Serenity pointed a finger out at the man and his son.

"Pleeeease!"

I placed her down and tugged at her fat cheeks.

"Serenity, Mommy needs a little quiet time right now."

I spread a thick blanket on the floor where she could sit and play. Then I pulled out my cellphone, which she'd cried for earlier along the drive to the country.

"Here. Play with this while Mommy thinks."

Ecstatic, Serenity grabbed the phone and immediately started punching buttons. It was only a matter of minutes before she was holding conversations with imaginary friends on the other line.

I sat on Mother's bed for over an hour and was grateful for the well-needed break from a city that echoed with laughter from uptown women carrying out their daily errands, some with babies hanging on their hips; the slam of dominoes on hard wood tables from men who had no fear in them, except that they dreaded going home to their wives; traffic lines that swelled before dawn, tires screeching, horns blowing, and a thick stench that hung in the air. Even when you couldn't smell it, you felt it. More than anything, I needed to get away from the ghost of the drunken boy I had surrendered my surname to.

Pain was stirring up from a heavy place within me. I was startled when I saw the broken and unnoticeable woman whose reflection beamed from the floor mirror across the room. I did manage to smile when I realized that I had finally lost the twenty pounds I wanted to get rid of. Still, I didn't have the appetite to entertain any form of therapy.

As I sat there thinking, I noticed Mother's old journal, still in the same place she'd rested it before she died. I wondered about the memories that lived in that book.

Curious, I took the book in hand and walked toward the window.

"Mommy, say hi to Martha!"

Serenity was still talking to an imaginary friend on the other line.

"Hi, Martha!" I said playfully, then handed the phone back to Serenity.

"Tell Martha Mommy has to do some reading, babe."

I listened to her tell Martha exactly that as I folded my tiny frame into the windowsill where the chatter on the phone, the chirping of the birds, the lad's laughter at the lakeside, and even the dog barking in the distance could not stir me away from what I was about to read. Mother loved to write, but I had not known the stories she never told until now. As I turned through the pages, by her penmanship alone, I could tell she was getting weaker over the months as she battled the vicious disease. While I read through her deepest kept secrets, I felt her humble presence:

Dear Diary, Nana always joked about how life was a landlord, and our souls were its tenants. And that one day we had to pay—with our last breath. I know I will pay soon, and right before life dims its lights, I will forgive the stranger who took my innocence and placed a permanent bitterness in my soul, staining an everlasting flame on the bed of my heart.

It's funny how life happens.

That I, in these last days, could live again, such is my dying wish. I have been to life. And life has been to me. Yet, I have driven away a part of me that I perhaps will never get back. I drove away my daughter. Not stopping to think that my own mother had done me the same.

Seems it was just yesterday I felt my newborn baby's soft hair pressed against my arms as I rode the filthy city bus through the biting winter cold to its last stop. A school-aged girl, perhaps my age, looked at me with a frown. Her mother turned her face, whispering something at her. I covered Ebony under a blanket and rocked her to sleep, hoping she would neither wake nor cry as the bus sunk and rose from every ditch in the well-traveled city streets. I was looked down upon—a young unwedded woman carrying a baby, nursing wounds within that no one would ever see. Wounds that would never heal.

My mother arranged for me to give away Ebony to a wealthy uptown woman who was barren. She convinced me that this would give me a second chance and I was affording Ebony a life I could never give her. She spouted at me harsh words and warned me not to say to anyone that I was raped, for they wouldn't believe me. Afraid of my mother, I agreed at first. Then one night, I gazed into my daughter's eyes and recognized the promise of life.

So perfect she was and is. So pure. How could sin have created something so promising? Why hath fate evoked a spate of mercy so great, it led to the birth of this miracle?

I felt the sting from my mother's palm against my face the entire ride. The blow from her hand was so powerful it knocked me to the floor.

The woman stood over me with fire in her eyes. Her hair was pulled back into a bun, just like the Huffingtons wore theirs. But she was far from a Huffington. Never good enough for my father—yet so perfect for him. She was furious at my change of heart not to give up Ebony.

I knew that to keep my child, I had to leave, and so I ran away.

A journey to nowhere makes you weary fast.

Rain caught me struggling through a dirty pathway with Ebony in hand. I came up on a shed behind an old wooden house with galvanized windows, and so I sought shelter there. Ebony managed to keep quiet the entire time but started wailing once the thunder began to roll.

"Young lady! What are you doing out there in the rain?" I was startled by a sharp voice that ringed through the storm.

By now, dark clouds blocked out the sunlight, and as the rain fell harder, streams of water flowed between the rocks, down to the muddy trail that led us to where we were.

A door swung open from the house in front of us, and an old lady in a white dress stood looking at us with hands on her hips. When I wouldn't answer, she disappeared into the house and five minutes later emerged with towels in her hands. She threw one over her head and walked over to us. Nervous, I thought to take off running. Just then, a flash of lightening reminded me that this was our only hope. Once she made her way over to us, she didn't speak a word. She threw a towel over my head, took Ebony in her arms, and wrapped her in the next towel.

I held on to Ebony's feet and the stout lady, no more than five feet, looked me in the eyes and in a thick West Indian accent said, "Well, you goin' let her catch cold and die?"

Still not trusting the stranger, I managed to let go of Ebony's feet, and the elderly woman led us into her home. I followed behind her, tiptoeing on one stone at a time, trying not to get my feet muddy.

It was warm indoors. Water was dripping from the roof, and someone was smart enough to place a bucket beneath the leakage to catch every drop. Every hour when the bucket filled, she exchanged it with another and pitched off the water into the backyard.

Not sure what to do, I watched along as she busied around the kitchen. She had a strong Carib-Indian build, with shiny dark skin and speckle-grey hair that was braided back in one big plait.

I didn't take my eyes off of her for too long. She lit the gasoline operated stove with a match. Ebony was still in her arms. The mystery woman then poured water into an iron pot and dropped a few leaves into it. As the water boiled, the house filled up with a minty scent.

My child didn't cry the entire time. Her eyes only danced around the cottage. Exhausted, I took a seat in an old rocking chair.

"Oh no, get up! You must change first! You're wet. Look over there, find a dress to change into!"

The old lady pointed to a closet in the corner. I eased out of the seat and walked over to the closet. The first piece of clothing I pulled out was a dress. I wasn't sure if she expected me to change right then and in front of her, but she was quick to confirm.

"Go ahead, change before you get sick!"

Embarrassed by my stretch marks and swollen breasts, I turned my back and changed as quickly as I could. Not long after, tea and warm garlic bread were prepared for me. She motioned me to sit at a small counter where a shaky wooden stool barely held my weight.

"You have formula for the baby?" she asked while sorting through a basket in the corner.

I sipped the hot mint tea and grimaced, then said no to her. She pulled out a knitted sweater that was apparently made for a baby, then on a table in the corner, wiped down Ebony and changed her into a warm sweater.

"Well, you will have to breastfeed her till morning."

Despite her stern tongue, she was warm-spirited. I could tell.

She let me eat, while she wiped down the counter and then cleaned the stove. Then once I was finished, she interrogated me.

"So what are you running from, young lady? And with a young baby at that?"

I swallowed hard, then shared my story with her. With one hand on her hip, she leaned against the wall and listened. Whether she believed me or not, she believed in me. The next morning, I woke up to find Ebony's clothes and my clothes hanging from a clothing line, drying in the faithful sunlight. That day she let me rest and fed and took care of the cheerful baby. The following day, she woke me up at five in the morning and said it was time to be a woman—whether or not I was ready.

In the coming weeks, she taught me to cook, clean, and how to handle a baby. She arranged a small room in one corner of the house for us. This particular room reeked of mothballs, but I didn't dare complain. The room didn't have a door either. Still, it was all the privacy I needed.

Three months had gone by, and she took the birth certificate I travelled with and enrolled me into a private school where she was friends with the head mistress. We kept up with the Sunday paper, and I was relieved to learn that there was no search for a missing Emily Huffington and baby. No one was looking for us. I came to know this old lady as Nana. She was a poor woman, but shared with us her last. We struggled together, we suffered together, and when things got better, we celebrated together. Ebony grew to favor Nana, even more than she resembled me. Both had rich chocolate skin tones and thick kinky hair that grew past their shoulders. An entire decade, and Nana treated us as her own. To me, she was an angel. Only that life always gets its way.

Diary, one peaceful evening, Nana, Ebony, and I gathered in the dining room for dinner. By now I had purchased a beautiful dining table for her as a gift once I completed my first novel and landed a contract from a publishing firm in the city. The table was placed directly beneath the roof that once leaked. I made sure that I'd repaired and remodeled the home for her and the roof was first on the list. Nana was proud of the new table, and in one day, she knitted a beautiful table runner that stretched from one end of the table to the next. She insisted we always sit at that table when we ate.

One Friday evening, Nana, with the help of Ebony, prepared dinner. What a mess my little Ebony made in the kitchen with the flour and sugar. Nana had taught her how to measure flour and what a pinch of salt meant. They fried up the best Johnny cakes I've ever had, and to this day Ebony is a great cook. We sat at the table like a family that evening. Nana was old but strong, with light brown eyes that searched your soul when she looked at you. She was intuitive and knew things without being told. She didn't speak much, but when she did her words were meaningful.

As we sat there, exchanging conversation, the front door opened. We were all surprised as none of us expected a visitor. Little Ebony, with a knife in one hand and fork in the next, continued dicing the steak on her plate. Just then, a towering man with a thick wild beard walked in. The look on Nana's face was one of terror, and in the same instance, my face matched hers.

It was him. Years had passed, and I was now a woman. I doubt he recognized me. But I could never forget that face. The moon was my only light that night. The only witness to the heartless crime. Ebony was the only proof of what had happened.

I flashed back to the struggle of me fighting off the stranger in the back seat of his wagon. That night, my mother was in a hurry to attend a party that she'd been invited to. Finally, an opportunity to appear among the elite and prove that she belonged. Maxwell Huffington would be there for sure, and maybe when he saw her in the arms of another, he would want her back. She spent her last on a beautiful shimmery navy-blue dress that fell gracefully to the floor. Her hair was straightened with a hot iron comb that she heated on the stove. I helped her to get dressed that night, and she was the most beautiful gem I'd ever seen.

"Hand me the red lipstick!"

She took her time applying her eyeliner while I shuffled nervously through a bag of foundations, face powders, mascaras, and eye shadows. I handed her the lipstick, and she snatched it from me, then lifted a bottle of whisky to her head before applying the paint to her lips.

I could smell the whisky then, as I sat in Nana's living room and the familiar stranger inched his way in. It took me back to my fully dressed mother, well-composed, not yet inebriated by her consumption of liquor. She was a professional travesty. The doorbell rang and her date for the night was standing on the other end. She never introduced me; I only glimpsed the fabric of his long trench coat and his large hands that held her waist line as he kissed her. In a low voice and unfamiliar accent, he told her she was beautiful. I stood in the hallway and watched, and without saying goodbye, she stepped out into the night with a new stranger.

I didn't mind being alone at thirteen. As long as I had pen and paper, I was okay. That night, I fell asleep while writing a poem, but was awoken by a deep voice rumbling over me in the dark.

"Wake up, sleeping beauty. Let's go get mommy."

The man with the accent I had heard earlier that evening, was now lifting me out of my mom's bed. I was confused but assumed my mom had arranged for him to come get me. Maybe the Huffingtons had sent for me and wanted me to join the other kids. If that wasn't the case, I wouldn't dare disrespect one of her friends, in fear that she would punish me severely. I pulled on a jacket, and we rode the elevator down to the first floor. His car was parked right in front of the building, and he signaled me to jump in.

"Where is my mom?" I asked. Careful not to sound too worried.

He laughed and caressed my face, "Mommy is waiting for us. Apparently, her invitation to this extravagant event was a mistake. Maxwell Huffington himself had us thrown out of the banquet hall."

He laughed about it and closed my door once I took a seat.

We drove deep into the city until I could no longer recognize the streets or stores we were passing. Several bars were still open, and I remember the car coming to a screeching halt when out of nowhere a drunken man appeared in the light, staggering across the road. Drunk as hell and with a cigar lit in one hand, my mother's friend cursed and spat at the man, then sped off. Soon he pulled over in a dark alley, where the moonlight peeped over at us from a tall, maybe thirteen-story building. He leaned over to touch me. With the doors locked, I leaped over to the back seat, hoping he wouldn't follow me there. And he did. As he unbuttoned his pants, all I could think of was Maxwell Huffington. The night he left us, he promised me that when I needed him the most, he would be there. My nails bore holes in the leather of the back seat as the stranger covered my mouth and crippled the little girl within me that night. When he was done, he threw a cloth at me and ordered me to wipe myself off quickly, then he drove me back to the apartment. I ran upstairs and took a long shower and hid my blood-stained underwear and clothing in my book bag and disposed of them the next day. About an hour later, I heard my mom's voice calling me as she entered through the door. I found her in the living room, drunk and on her knees, red lipstick smeared across her face, mascara dragged to her cheeks.

"Help me up, girl!"

I ran over to help her to her feet. She fell twice and each time I struggled to help her up. I rested her in bed, removed her heels and her dress, and helped her into a robe. She leaned over the bed and threw up on the carpet, then looked at me with a smirk and said, "I ain't good enough for those people. That makes you no good either."

She drew herself back onto the bed and mockingly said, "Never was. Never will be."

In no time, she was sound asleep.

"Stephen…Son. It's been years."

Nana didn't move from her seat. The intruder in the living room was no stranger at all.

I swallowed a hard knot down my throat. The man who took my innocence had a name. How was it that fate had led me to this tiny cottage? The same place Ebony's dad had been raised. How was it that Nana, such a dignified woman, had given birth to a menace?

Without an explanation, I left that night with me and Ebony's *life crammed in the back seat of the noisy car I purchased from a mechanic on Auburn Street—a small neighborhood in the country, not too far from where we lived. Nana had never seen me like this, and she begged me not to leave. With whatever came over me, I packed quickly and had Ebony kiss Nana goodbye.*

I will never know what I ran away from the night I left home.

A few years later, I mailed off a letter to Nana and enclosed a check to help and to compensate her for her kindness. How stupid was I to think I could ever repay her?

A week after, a letter came back with the same check enclosed and a note.

"I knew it," she said.

"I believed you. And the moment I saw Ebony, I knew she was my blood, even without knowing. In these last days, there's nothing money can buy for a dying lady. Send me your prayers."

Nana wrote once a week after that, for two years straight, and then the letters stopped coming. I never wrote back.

I pulled my eyes away from the diary briefly, to think of my dear Nana. I wondered if she died alone too. I was still seated in the windowsill, and my Serenity was now soundly sleeping on the bed with my phone still pressed to her ears. The father and son were no longer fishing at the lakeside, and the dogs had retired their barks.

As I continued to turn the pages of her diary, tears welled up in my eyes. I knew now why we never saw Nana again. I thought, how long these roads we take may seem, yet life's still shorter. I flipped to the last page of her diary, which read:

Life is such a funny thing. Ebony happened to me. Cancer happened to me. Life just happens to us. I suffered long. I made good and bad choices, and so did Ebony. Like time, she was a teacher. And I became the student. I learned to love. I learned to hold on. I learned to let go. I learned how to become. If only I now had time to put it all into play. Plenty of times I question who I am. I'm not sure if I am Nana's daughter, but I am certain that I'm my daughter's mother.

As I placed the diary down and made my way over to Serenity to hold her in my arms, I realized who I was and where I fit in the dangerous cycle of drunken men and women who were forced to make painful choices. I was the mistakes they made and didn't make. I was Nana's guilt for a son she chased away. I was a drunken woman's hope to be seen and accepted by a husband who had rejected her. I was a father's broken promise. We happened to each other. A part of me died that eerie night when Mother took her last breath. But that she'd witnessed my first breath, and I her last, was worth celebrating. Had I the opportunity to walk in her shoes I would've taken the same old dirty path that led her to Nana's cottage, where she gave me the gift of love. At that moment, everything in me knew I had my own battles to fight. It was time to clean the dirty house I seldom visited and make it my home.

Over the next few weeks, with the help of Natalia to whom I had reached out for help, I polished up the lakeside mansion, changed the linens in every room, and placed up new curtains. Natalia spent some nights with us, and while we didn't keep much conversation, we always ate dinner together. One particular night, I did a fish fry, fresh Johnny cakes, and red snapper just as Nana had taught me to make them.

"Mmmm. These are good! Ms. Huffington was not kidding. You're a good cook!" Natalia spoke with a mouth full of food and a snapper tail between her fingers.

I was pleased to know she enjoyed my food, but was all the more grateful to see how loving and careful she was with Serenity, who often followed her around the house asking question after question. At times, I sat in the room and listened to Natalia as she patiently responded to each and every question. She was more patient than I was for sure.

Since Natalia spent so much time with us, I told her that Lady China was more than welcome. The next day, she brought the cat over and to my surprise, the furry animal became Serenity's best friend. Both Natalia and I were relieved as the child's attention was now fixed on the playful pet. Slowly but surely, the home was filling up with life and laughter.

Some mornings, I clipped fresh flowers from the garden and placed them in vases throughout the house. My favorite was a bouquet of long-stemmed gladiolus that I had made into a perfect centerpiece for the dining table.

I took Serenity for plenty of strolls through the courtyard, one of Mother's favorite places to sit and meditate. It was on one quiet afternoon, while Natalia was out doing errands and I had taken Serenity for a walk through the courtyard, that I stumbled upon a worn-out bench with two wine glasses leaned against it and an empty vintage wine bottle, half-buried in mud. I didn't think much of it, until one evening after I had put Serenity to sleep, I heard a knock on the door. By the time I made it down, a tall man dressed in white was already walking away to his car.

"Hey!" I called at him, but he didn't turn around.

Off to the side was a box that he apparently had placed there. On the top of the box was a note that simply said, My darling Erica Forbes. I kneeled down to open up the box, and my ears followed the Corvette's engine as it disappeared into the spring evening. Within the box was everything I needed. Layers of glimmering hope that my mother did live after all. Black and white photos of her and a tall, attractive man—the same man I had seen at the funeral. Thousands of stories told through photos. Vineyards they visited, oceans they sailed, weekend trips to cabins in the woods, summer picnics right on the courtyard bench. Hugs in mint coats beneath the Eiffel Tower. How long was I away from her that I missed these significant parts of her life? He was the inspiration for some of her bestselling novels, I could tell. I thought to myself, *funny how strangers bring the best gifts.*

The courtyard bench became my new place of retreat. Every evening until the summer ended, I sat and flipped through photos of a woman I never knew lived and read through a box of Nana's letters I'd stumbled upon while cleaning. I read through every letter until I found my grandmother's last words.

> *My greatest wish is that you my daughters find peace. Dying is what the living do, so live a little. Love a lot. Find laughter in your pain. Search for light in the dark; for even the light needs darkness from which to shine.*

Destiny Hemphill

Destiny Hemphill is a poet currently based in Durham, North Carolina. Her work has appeared in *Narrative Northeast, Scalawag,* and *Button Poetry.*

SO THE SHIP WAS LIKELY TO BE BROKEN

every morning i practice
releasing you
from my spirit
and there are some days
that i have convinced myself
that i have learned
but dusks like these
when i am still

i feel a tornado whirring within me
with remnants of you in its midst

you know
before i was born
when i was still in my mother's womb
a prophetess came
and pressed her palm
against my mother's belly
and pronounced
"a storm is coming"
so my mother was not afraid
nor surprised
when it rained for
ten days before i was born
and when it rained for ten days after

and when they pulled me
from between my mother's legs and
she smelled the permanence
of loneliness
on my skin
she said, "this is good." and
when she heard
in the labor of my breathing
the inheritance
of the tempest
in my soul
and in my bones

and underneath my fingertips
she whispered,
"peace.
may you always know
when
and how
to be still."

and you could feel it, couldn't you
the surge of lightning
when we placed our palms
against each other's to pray
the way the supplications
seemed to always thunder
in my throat
seemed to scare you
convinced you that
i was drowning within myself
no matter how often
i told you
that i am simply
my own holy
baptism

i said: i feel like all tornado
in this heart
beneath these ribs of mine
i didn't have much space
for you
without crowding myself out
without causing my heart to swell
but i stretched for you,
i did
and i have the bruises to prove it

i said: i stretched for you
i did,
and i have the debris
left over
from us
to prove it

look…i know what it's like
to have stuff rotting inside of you
so entangled and hard to pull out
right after something hurts you so bad
that it's unspeakable
and a portion of your spirit simply
wastes away
i just wanted to flush you out
and i know what it's like
to try to die unto yourself
but you never become renewed
you just stay dead
and you walk around
searching for somebody
to unbury you from the tomb
you call your skin
the storm within me
just wanted to cleanse you

i wanted to water you
i wanted to watch you grow
until one day i had to wonder:
how long could i be committed to your growth—
when my reservoirs are drying up,
when my gardens are wilting?

and i know, i know
i'm trying to be still
but it feels like too much like last time
too much like
not me, not again
not me, not again
like too much land
and not enough sea
like too much desert
and not enough rainwater
too much
i need space in this heart of mine
cuz there's not enough moon
not enough stars
not enough galaxy

40 AND . . .

incorruptible
unemployed
unloved

and African
a woman

coveted
emulated
rejected

uncompromising
childhood-robbed, childless
and seemingly careless
proud and betrayed

40
just a scarring number
on the wrinkles of years
and wrinkling years
yet not scared

brutally 40 after a tornado of struggling days
a fortress of bitter souvenirs
unforgettable
a slice of African feminine
fable — unforgiving as a human being

40 as the endurance
of enmity and environing insecurity

40 years of unlearned wisdom and unleashed but unrequited love
for love drives people away
love isn't contagious and it doesn't pay
in today's s & m lust get-aways

40 units of 52-week periods of intensive unrewarded labor

and hopes degraded encore
and encore
without killing the core of an African woman
 40
still
Ready to live
rather than survive in mediocrity

Stay free.

Your ancestors

Andria Nacina Cole

Andria Nacina Cole was raised in a house full of women and learned everything worth knowing about storytelling from their mouths. Lots of practice and careful study, supplemented a wee bit, by degrees in creative writing from Morgan State and Johns Hopkins Universities, have helped her land short stories in *Baltimore City Paper, The Feminist Wire,* and *Hamilton Stone Review,* among others. Ploughshares recently published her novella *Men Be Either Or, But Never Enough* and she is the recipient of five Maryland State Arts Councils awards. She is co-founder of the critical reading and writing program, A Revolutionary Summer, which exposes young black women to womanist literary giants in an effort to push them headfirst into self-love. Andria Nacina Cole resides in Baltimore, Maryland.

THE GORGEOUS WORD NO

Having survived invisibility (for he never claimed me).
Having survived infidelity (the sort where he never ever stops/the women never ever run out—it is like he is a tall/wide/hungry sponge and they are all the five oceans).
Having survived his hands wrapped 'round my neck (you have not been choked, honey, 'less you've called God and heard nothing for an answer).
Having survived the sacred word *bitch*.
And the other one *whore*.
And the other other one *slut*.
Said with such power I thought they were my daddy-given names.

Having survived invisibility, because he never claimed me. HaveIsaidthat?

And two tattoos, because one wasn't telling enough. (I told the fat tattoo lady, "Won't you make his name look like love?" She said, "What color is that?" But I ain't know. "Just 'long as you make it big and spell it right.")

Having survived her scent. And her scent. And hers.

Having survived silence (he was always gone).
And Excedrin (whole bottles at a time).
And lala land (this is where you live when every word's a lie).

Having survived my daughter's questions tripped out her eyes, then chasing me 'round and 'round the room.

Having survived no marriage and I didn't even know I wanted to be married.
And the realization that there, in his particular corner of the world, I was nobody.

Having survived being turned to stone (the body calluses in an effort to protect the soft parts—look at your hands, for instance).

And turning out a mean/however pretty, bitch (sacred).

And. doing. to. him. most. everything. he. did. to. me.

For the feeling, baby.

The power.

Having survived three thousand days, no sun/little water/mere sips of breath.

Having fashioned from the story a rock (jagged) where a heart should go, I've come to know some things.

Four of them are:

1. You are responsible for yourself. If you don't realize this until age 50, things will be tough. So what you reached out to him purely and with only kindness in your heart? Said, "I love you sugar" and meant it, and showed it, and never ever crossed him? Your intentions don't shield you from the appropriate consequence. You are not special in that way. You are special in another. If you wait on him to treat you right, you are a gambler. And you will lose much.

2. That you are good does not guarantee another's goodness. They did not spare Jesus Christ. What do you think they'll do with you? Sometimes goodness is no match for intelligence. It is no match for action. For self-preservation. For determination. For the gorgeous word no.

3. It is never ever too late to leave.

4. It is never ever too early either.

ENCOMIUM: A MANUMITTED SCREAM

I am
Negro, the genuine
Hero
Of my recalcitrant ruin

I am
The Negro, the genius
Of my battles
Wrecked and dismantled
Forever prostrated
By my brothers of hell
And erotic betrayals

Loss…
Dust glitter;
Tossed and lustered litter…
Chartered memories
Of manumitted aftermath…
The skimmed Dream, in a bribe,

Has embittered
Its voluptuous mocha

i,
woman
and civilized Negro
of slavish
Money-maker tribes,

Live
In hope of a reiterated scream:

Negroism needs heroism!!

BLACK DEATH

I need to talk about how no one is talking about
the elephant in the room
the big, bleeding, black elephant in the room
that trampled my rose colored glasses underfoot

I need to talk about how no one is talking about
Black Death
septic not skeptic Black Death
deep-seated, mistreated Black Death

I need to change my voicemail greeting to
"can't come to the phone right now" because I'm grieving
set my Out of Office reply to "I've suffered a loss"
I am at a loss for words

water Cooler Talk is Jen and Ben
Courtney and Scott
who cares?
Kimye? I'm not ok

see, I can't make the meeting today
because I'm screaming in my car
sobbing at the nightly news
shrieking at the radio
singing a spiritual in the shower

fearing the Grim Reaper is my black brothers' keeper
scythe blocking the light from reaching my eyes
this old genocide a rolling blackout
and I can't shout else I'm an angry black woman
any gross old epithet to make me less human

I need to talk about
Trayvon, Mike Brown, Marissa Alexander, Sandra Bland
am I standing in quicksand?
because I swear I'm sinking

I need to talk about
this living nightmare
being black in America in 2015
where hoarders of historical hate
fly Confederate banners of evil
that laugh in the sky above
pyres of black smoke
from black bodies

I need to talk about
how can you function?
what's it like to function amid the forever funereal?

I don't want to function at the junction
of ignorance plus privilege
if at the corner of apathy and apartheid
is where I must meet you
then I will never attend
my soul hasn't had a chance to mend

does it not give you pause?
not even a moment of silence
no grief counselor in sight
ignoring.

people talk sardonically about a quarter life crisis
saying millennials aged 25 are
too anxious about making the wrong move
that we don't move
but I can't move because I don't want to get shot
can't move because I have not forgotten
can't move because I...I... dot dot dot

hands up, eyes down, mouth quivering to stay shut
holding back an Edvard Munch type scream
bursting at the seams
torn between wanting to be alive
and wanting to dive below the surface

I want to extract the empathy from you like rainwater from a cactus

when my kin wrinkle like raisins in the sun
modern day bullet wounds akin to being hung
strange fruit are the media's loot
demonizing the dead on CNN
innocence is a death sentence

headlines of "black killers" oppose "white shooters"
"mentally ill" versus "society's ills"
diction dictates decorum
diction dictates dissent
diction the prescription for my malaise
the black mayonnaise that coats my days
all the while I can't catch my breath
can't ignore Black Death

I

CAN'T

BREATHE.

IF NOT YOU - THEN WHO?!

They cried out one day
From beyond the grave
With whispers distant
That said-
"Restore us to our rightful place"
If not you - then who?
Who shall carry legacy on shoulders
Who shall carry traditions passed over?
Who shall stride and bear the name?
You must reach the promised land
For the past generations who couldn't complete
For you, my dear, must complete this thing
Who shall continue on?
Who shall carry the torch for the unborn?
Who shall lead and pursue?
Who shall accomplish tasks that we alone couldn't do?
The legacy has been forthright and passed on to you
For you, dear, must do what you alone have been born to do
Create
Birth
Walk next to destiny
Climb mountains and defeat obstacles
If not you - then who?!
Who shall leave lasting imprints that we couldn't do?
Death came ripe but the legacy now has been passed onto you
We fought hard for the position that we have handed to you
If not you - then who?!
Who shall bear the mark of our legacy?
Who shall strive on with endurance?
Who shall defeat generational obstacles?
Who shall march on just a little more wiser?
Who has been birthed to complete the assignment?
If not you, my dear - then who?!
Your lineage cries out for you to walk and carry the torch
So pursue!
If not you - then who?!

I KNOW A BURNING BUSH WHEN I SEE ONE

this is the function of violence:
to persuade you to shackle
your own tongue
chain it
until it atrophies
train it
to recoil from words
make you consider swallowing it
cutting it out
because after so long--
what else is there to say?
aren't the words all used up?
and cut off your hands
cuz you're tired of digging graves
and set yourself ablaze,
forget the sackcloth:
you'll become the ashes
you'll return to dust
you don't remember what being dust feels like
but you do know what it is to be trampled on
still you can't say you remember
what being dust feels like
but you know
that's the point
you don't remember how it feels
yet here your tongue revolts
and you will honor the blackness they call thug
the divinity they call perversity
the sacred they
say is unholy
the sacred they say
is unholy
the sacred they say is
unholy
ain't it something how
they say our sacred is unholy
yet they stay sacrificing us

makes you wonder
what heaven are they seeking
when this shedding of blood
this splitting of bone
this scarring of flesh
this caustic bleaching
is none righteous

REDEMPTION OF MAMMY

They didn't realize who you were
Your powerful waves of
Nurture
An enigma
Your ability to care for so many
Amazing and intimidating
Mami Mommi
Mami Wata
Yemoja
During the horrific Maafa
You delivered healthy babies
And healed with herbs and bark
You
The power behind the plantation
Your deceptive smile
and
Willing service
perceived as loyalty
While you fed Turner and Vesey
And gave Prosser the keys to the
Big house
Nurtured their plans for liberation
Old wicked Mammy
Who nursed young masta
Who nursed Dessalines
And prepared his herbal packets
for battle
Playing both sides
Our brilliant Iya
So we would survive
to tell the truth
about you
about the magic in your big, full arms
We survived because
of your
Intuitive and tempestuous skill
We redeem you Mammy
We redeem you today

Donna McGregor Hall

Born in the Bronx, New York, to Jamaican parents, Donna was sent to Jamaica at the age of two months to be raised by her grandparents in St. Ann, Jamaica. At the age of nine, Donna's mother sent for her to return to the United States. Since then Donna has attended and worked for Howard University, become a real estate agent and broker, and a singer, songwriter, model, and mother. She writes songs and poetry and collaborates heavily with other musical artists performing at music conferences nationally. Donna is currently working on a music video for International House Music artist Biblical Jones with his song entitled "Blowing in the Wind."

BLACK

Black is my refuge—Black is my song
Black is my comfort—when things go wrong
Black is my beauty—Black is my pride
Black is the color—beautiful night
Black is my refuge—Black is my song
Black is my comfort—when things go wrong
Black is my beauty—Black is my pride
Black is the color—when you go inside
Black is my being—Black is my soul
Black is my solace—I'm in control
Without and with nothing
In void of the light
Black is inside me—Black is my light.

RECALLING ORIGINS: THE BLENDING OF BLUE WATERS

This is a symbolic ritual for mothers and daughters to maintain unity and a healthy bond in both difficult and uplifting times. It is a ritual to celebrate their shared journey and larger connection to women throughout the world.

Gather the names of the female members in your ancestral line who lived good lives, reflected love and nurtured themselves, their families, and their communities. This is a time to bring positive affirmations about being a mother or a daughter to the table. Be generous in your words and affirmations. Be highly complimentary in your reflections of one another and your female lineage.

Supplies

- One large clear glass vase
- Two wine glasses
- Bottle of sparkling white grape juice
- Large clear glass bowl
- Seven crystal beads
- Silver beads
- Gallon of spring water
- Blue seven-day candle
- White flowers with ample-sized petals
- White tablecloth
- Two comfortable chairs

Burn a stick of Egyptian Musk, Frankincense, or Myrrh (you can choose another, but be certain it is natural and pleasing to the senses). The incense will purify the area in which you will place your ritual table. Place a small table in a quiet and undisturbed place in your home. Cover it with a white tablecloth. Fill your large clear glass vase with tap water and grace the table with white flowers. Next, place the seven crystals and seven sterling silver or stainless steel beads in the large clear glass bowl and fill it with spring water. Place your wine glasses on the table and have your favorite incense handy. Place the chilled white sparkling grape juice on the table, too.

For seven days in the evening, perhaps after dinner or before you turn in for bed, sit at your table and meditate with one another. Meditate on the beautiful experience of being a mother or a daughter. Dim the lights. Have your affirmations ready. Light the blue candle and place it behind the bowl of water. Light your incense. Make your shrine beautiful—a place where you enjoy sitting and reflecting.

Talk about the positive attributes of women in your lineage. Pray for strength and unity for your mother-daughter bond. Pray for strength and light for the women in your family. Sing or speak a chant for Yemaya. Take time to sit quietly with your mother or daughter if you can. Breathe, pray, reflect on the best of yourselves. Dip your fingertips in the bowl occasionally and spray the water around you to refresh the space to remind you that you are tapping into Yemaya's energy and asking for her blessing on your divine feminine bonds. Near the close of your ritual, share a cool drink of sparkling grape juice. Reflect on the foam that trims Yemaya's shores and be rejuvenated. You will know when it is time to close the ritual. Put out your candle. Wash your wine glasses and put away your sparkling white grape juice for the following evening's ritual. Clean the incense burner. Each day freshen the water in the vase for the flowers and the water in the glass bowl that holds the crystal and silver.

At the conclusion of the seven days, journal your thoughts, inspirations, and spiritual experiences during the ritual. How have you been elevated in your role as a mother, daughter, and person? What other insights did you glean from this spiritual work?

I trust Yemaya will lift and bring light and joy to all the women who partake in this ritual in her honor.

Ase!

Janine Jackson

Janine Jackson is from South Florida. She is a creative consultant that has created in various aspects for more than 10 years, using acrylic paints, illustration software applications, and image-editing programs. She develops images that focus on the power and beauty found in life. Jackson's graphic work serves as the cover visual for *Sistah Vegan: Black Female Vegans Speak on Food, Identity, Health, and Society*. Her vector imagery appears within the 33rd Edition of *We'Moon* (Radical Balance | 2014). Additional works are featured within online publications such as *Corset Magazine*, the *Global Fund for Women's Imagining Equality*, and print publications like *Spirituality & Health Magazine*.

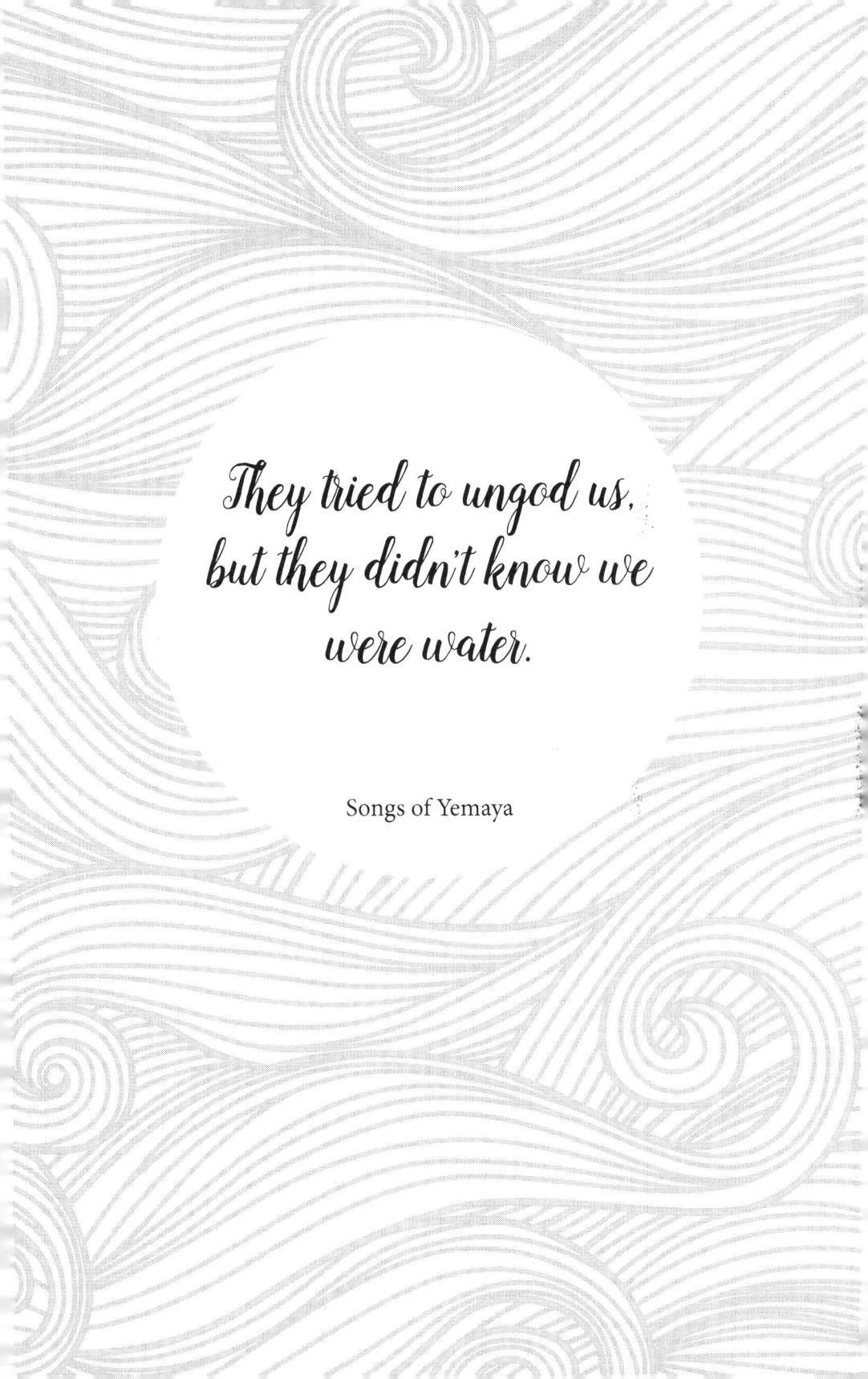

They tried to ungod us, but they didn't know we were water.

Songs of Yemaya